Jesus at the home of his parents
Painting by John Millais—1850

JESUS OF NAZARETH

THE COVER

The cover image is the Chi-Rio, which depicts the first two letters of Christ in the Greek alphabet. According to the church historian Eusebius, this is the sign that Constantine had his soldiers paint on their shields, just as he had seen in a vision with the words, "In this sign conquer."

DEDICATION

This book is dedicated to my daughter Gwendolyn Chantini, who encouraged me to rush in where angels fear to tread.

ACKNOWLEDGMENT

I am deeply indebted to Dr. Paul L. Maier for his patient editing and critique of the manuscript. He devoted far more time than warranted to my meager attempts to produce a readable book, and if it has any merit at all, it is due to his tireless reviews.

JESUS OF NAZARETH

OTHER BOOKS BY CHARLES DAUDERT

In the Wake of the Northern Lights

The Bridge Monkey

The Temptation of St. Rosalie

Andrew Durnford, Portrait of a Black Slave Owner

The Narrative of John Tanner, The Falcon

The Metamorphsis, translation with commentary

Off the Record with Martin Luther, translation with commentary

First Let's Kill all the Lawyers

The Pilgrim's Progress, Modern English Edition with commentary

The Historical Perspective

ABOUT THE AUTHORS

Charles Daudert graduated *magna cum laude* from Western Michigan University. He received the degree of Juris Doctor from Wayne State University Law School at the head of his class. After a successful career as a trial lawyer, he retired to write full time. He is the author of several fiction and non-fiction books, as well as magazine articles and short stories.

Benjamin Rush Rhees, an ordained Baptist, was the president of the University of Rochester from 1900 to 1935. He is known primarily for *The Life of Jesus of Nazareth, a Study.* Although the writing is often difficult to follow, Rhees' work is a neglected masterpiece, far surpassing many of the more modern studies of the life of Jesus of Nazareth. The more noteworthy passages from his "*Study*" have been preserved in this edition, after substantial editing and re-writing.

Paul L. Maier, author and professor of ancient history, is a graduate of Harvard (M.A.) and Concordia Seminary, St. Louis. He received the Doctor of Philosophy degree *summa cum laude* from the University of Basel, Switzerland. He is the author of numerous books on Christianity, including the Gold Medallion award-winning book *Josephus: The Essential Writings.* Several million of Dr. Maier's books are in print in a dozen languages, as well as more than 200 scholarly articles in professional journals. Dr. Maier is also second vice president of the Lutheran Church, Missouri Synod.

JESUS OF NAZARETH

TABLE OF CONTENTS

The Historical Perspective

JESUS OF NAZARETH

JESUS OF NAZARETH

INTRODUCTION

More books have been written about Jesus of Nazareth than anyone who has ever lived. Do we really need another?

Quite arguably, we do, and for several reasons. New historical research and archaeological findings always add significant brush strokes to the traditional portrait of Jesus. More importantly, however, is the necessity to clean that portrait from the grime that has been deposited on it by radical scholars over the past decades who have besmirched the image of Christ into caricature..

These pages aid the restorative process. The author is not a theologian or clergyman but a lawyer with a gift for uncovering evidence, a talent so vital to his craft. As many others have before him, he has joined in the search for the historical Jesus, but his methodology is more honest and credible than that of many other searchers for whom the sensational overrules the factual.

In the case of Jesus, presenting historical *fact*, not reconstructed fantasy, is the aim of Charles Daudert's research and his purpose in writing this book. And here, he correctly observes that—far more than any other religious system in the world—Christianity's Holy Book deals in fact—solid, sober fact—in its historical segments. Only one other religion in the world can also make that claim, since its Holy Book is similarly factual, and that is Christianity's parent, namely Judaism. Quite obviously, its *Hebrew Bible*, known by Christians as the Old Testament, also has claim to strong credentials. Christianity's, however, are even stronger, since its New Testament is nearer to our own time and thus has the advantage of many more correlations between its internal evidence and the external testimony of geography, archaeology, ancient history, and other disciplines.

In a courtroom, hard fact about a case should be the deciding concern, not subjective "massaging" of fact to suit the purposes of a client. The same should certainly be true in the court of world opinion regarding religion. Amid the welter of competing spiritualities today with holy books invented by founders with claimed revelations, the credentials of Christianity and its sources in the Old and New Testaments are exponentially more reliable accounts of what actually happened to real people at real places during real times in the past.

These are more than idle claims, since the evidence can be tested and corroborated by abundance of information from the contemporary world of antiquity.

Here is just one example of many that could be cited. In Luke's Gospel, it is reported that the preaching of John the Baptist, as a prelude to the public ministry of Jesus, began at a specific time and place in history: "In the fifteenth year of Tiberius Caesar [A.D. 28/29], when Pontius Pilate was governor of Judaea [A.D. 26-36], Herod tetrarch of Galilee, his brother Philip tetrarch of the lands of Ituraea and Trachonitis, Lysanias tetrarch of Abilene, during the highpriesthood of Annas and Caiaphas, the word of God came to John son of Zechariah, in the wilderness " (Luke 3:1). Within a year, Luke tells us, John the Baptist is arrested, beheaded, and the torch is passed to Jesus of Nazareth, whom John baptized in the River Jordan.

How many of these names mentioned by Luke were actual people? All of them! Tiberius Caesar certainly existed and his reign is well documented in Roman history. Pontius Pilate was the prefect (governor) of Judea, and the cornerstone of a building he constructed in Caesarea in honor of Tiberius, with both their names on it, was discovered there.

JESUS OF NAZARETH

Herod Antipas (son of Herod the Great) was the Roman puppet ruler of Galilee, his brother Philip ruler of those lands today known as the Golan Heights. Annas and Caiaphas were high priests at Jerusalem. Their historical personalities were described in detail by Flavius Josephus, the contemporary Jewish historian; and Caiaphas's own bones were discovered in an ossuary with his name inscribed on it in 1990. Could there be harder physical evidence than this?

John, also prominently mentioned by Josephus, baptized in the River Jordan, which flows on today, while Jesus of Nazareth is certainly an equally historical personage, as attested by major sources also outside the New Testament, such as the Roman historians Tacitus, Suetonius and Pliny; rabbinical traditions referring to Y'shua ha Notzri (Jesus of Nazareth in Aramaic), as well as Josephus—not one of these sources Christian. An entire chapter could be devoted to this passage alone. Accordingly, the sources Daudert uses for this book are impeccable, a series of "smoking guns" from the past that would convince any jury in the world.

But how does this author handle these sources? Every book on Jesus ever written will offer varying interpretations of the evidence, but this study avoids the extremes to which Jesus scholarship has been subjected over the past decades.

Is this, then, *the* definitive work on Jesus? No, certainly not. Such a work will likely have to await the return of Jesus himself. Will readers concur with every point the author raises regarding "the greatest life ever lived"? No. certainly not. Yet reading these pages will prove eminently worthwhile, if only to see how the luminous life of Jesus is refracted by this particular prism to show some hues that are well known, others less known, and still others, new and

fresh.
　This is how Jesus affects people to the present day.

—Paul L. Maier
Author and Professor of Ancient History
Western Michigan University

The Historical Perspective

PREFACE

The purpose of this book is to make the Scriptures "come alive" by tying the stories of the Bible closely to the well-known people and events of the time. For example, we all know the story of Jesus' birth at Bethlehem, but how many of us realize that Herod the Great, who ruled over Judea when Jesus was born, was put upon the throne by the Roman General Mark Antony, and that Antony and Cleopatra committed suicide less than 25 years before Jesus was born.

And how many of us realize that many of the Palestinians of the West Bank are actually Jews. They are descendants of the Samaritans, the Jews of the North, who converted to Islam, and, thus, are descendants of the original 12 tribes of Israel, and brothers of their neighboring Jews.

History buffs looking for more detailed information on the life of Jesus and the early Church will find the sources quoted in this book to be rich, rewarding and reliable. Others, whose curiosity regarding Jesus and the early Christians may have been aroused by popular movies or television programs, but who are overwhelmed by Bibles consisting of 2000 pages of small print, will find this book a comfortable place to begin.

And many firm Christian believers, who have never heard of Josephus or Eusebius, will find this book to be a good introduction to those works, and come away with a compelling urgency to read further in them.

An additional purpose of this book is to shed light upon certain accounts in the New Testament which have been a source of anti-Semitism. For example, the Jews are often condemned for having chosen Barabbas over Jesus when Pilate offered to free a prisoner. However, this could just as easily have been a case of mistaken identity.

In the Chronology and text of this book, dates are used with the designation BC (Before Christ) and AD (from the Latin "anno Domini," year of our Lord). This practice is no longer considered "politically correct." Modern writers now use the term BCE (before the common era), in place of BC, and the designation CE (common era), in place of AD. However, with apologies to anyone whose sensibilities may be offended, this book continues to use the older designations as the change which is taking place has not yet become commonly accepted and the new designations of BCE and CE seem to create more confusion than their use warrants.

The Historical Perspective

CHRONOLOGY

1850 BC   -Abraham arrives in Canaan to secure the land for his descendants as directed by Yahweh (Genesis 12).

1700   -Joseph sold by his brothers. His father and the rest of the family follow him to Egypt. The sons of Israel are forced into slavery by the Egyptians.

1250   -The Exodus led by Moses.

1200   -Joshua invades Palestine.

1000   -David captures Jerusalem.

957-   -Solomon builds the First Temple at Jerusalem

586   -Deportation of the Jews of Judah to Babylon. The Temple at Jerusalem and the city are destroyed.

539   -Cyrus, King of the Persians, conquers Babylon.

538   -By edict of Cyrus, the Jews are re turned from exile.

JESUS OF NAZARETH

520-515   -Building of the Second Temple.

336-323   -Conquests of Alexander the Great.

319   -Ptolemy, a successor general of Alexander, becomes King of Egypt and takes over rule of Judea.

143   -The Jews establish their independence under the leadership of Judas Maccabaeus (see the books of Maccabees).

63   -The Roman General Pompey conquers Jerusalem.

49   -Julius Caesar seizes power in Rome.

47   -Julius Caesar names Herod military governor.

44   -Julius Caesar is assassinated.

40   -Herod flees to Rome during a revolt aided by the Parthians (Persians) and is declared king of Judea by the Romans.

37   -Roman forces recapture Jerusalem and Mark Anthony returns Herod to the throne.

31   -Octavian (Emperor Caesar Augustus)

	defeats Mark Antony and Cleopatra at the naval battle of Actium.
30	-Antony and Cleopatra commit suicide. Egypt becomes a Roman province.
06	-John the Baptist is born at Aim Karim, about 5 miles west of Jerusalem.
	-Jesus is born in Bethlehem.
04	-Herod the Great dies. Jesus is about two years old.
	-Caesar Augustus divides Herod's Kingdom among his three sons. Archelaus is given Judea and Samaria. Herod Antipas is given Galilee and Perea. Philip is given the remaining territories.
	-Mary, Joseph and Jesus return to Nazareth from Egyptian exile after learning of Herod's death.
01 AD	The turn of the century and the first year of the common era, designated by CE, mistakenly reported as the year of the birth of Jesus.
05	-Birth of Paul at Tarsus. Paul is about ten years younger than Jesus.

JESUS OF NAZARETH

06	-Caesar banishes Herod's son Archelaus to Gaul because of his incompetent administration. Rome takes over direct control of the government, and the first Roman prefect (governor) is sent to Judea.
	-Revolt in Galilee followed by widespread revolt in Judea. The Romans burn Sepphoris, the capital of Galilee, then proceed to Jerusalem and put down the revolt there. Jesus is about 11 years old. In the following years, Herod Antipas rebuilds Sepphoris, likely providing employment for Joseph and his son, Jesus, the carpenters from Nazareth, about an hour's journey away.
07	-Jesus discusses scripture with the doctors of law at the Temple, about age 12.
14	-Roman Emperor Augustus (Octavian) dies, Tiberius becomes emperor and rules until 37 AD.
26	-Pontius Pilate appointed prefect (governor) of Judea.
29	-Autumn, Jesus is baptized by John the Baptist and begins his mission.

The Historical Perspective

30   -Early, Jesus returns to Galilee from
          Judea after the temptation in the wil-
          derness, and settles in Capernaum.

          -The first Passover that Jesus is in Jeru-
          salem during his ministry.

          -The expulsion of the money-changers
          from the Temple.

31   -Early, John the Baptist is beheaded.

          -Jesus visits Nazareth and teaches in
          the synagogue.

32   -Jesus in Jerusalem for the Feast of
          Tabernacles.

          -Jesus returns to Jerusalem for the
          Feast of Dedication (Hanukah).

          -The resurrection of Lazarus at Beth-
          any.

33   -Jesus enters Jerusalem as the Messiah.

          -Jesus returns to Jerusalem for the
          Passover.

          -The Last Supper.

-Jesus is crucified by Pontius Pilate.
-The Resurrection and the empty tomb.

36   -Pilate recalled to Rome.

-Martyrdom of Stephen, Paul's conversion.

37   -Caligula becomes emperor at Rome and remains in power until 41.

-Paul in Arabia, then Damascus.

-The Jewish historian, Josephus is born.

39   -Paul escapes from Damascus and visits the elders of the Church.

41   Caligula assassinated and Claudius becomes emperor.

43   -Paul and Barnabas at Antioch. Peter in Samaria.

45   -Letter of James

45   -Beginning of first mission of Paul.

49   -End of Paul's first mission.

The Historical Perspective

50	-Oral tradition of the gospel is put into written form as the Aramaic Matthew.
	-Beginning of second mission of Paul. Letters to the Thessalonians.
52	-End of second mission of Paul.
53	-Beginning of Paul's third mission. Letter to the Philippians. 1 Corinthians. Letter to the Galatians. 2 Corinthians.
54	-Nero becomes emperor and remains in power until 68.
57-58	-Paul at Corinth. Letter to the Romans.
	-James, the brother of the Lord, heads the Christian community at Jerusalem.
58-59	-Paul a captive at Caesarea.
60	-Paul's voyage to Rome.
	-Paul in Rome under military guard. Letters to Colossians, Ephesians, Philemon and Philippians.
62	-The High Priest Ananias has James, the brother of the Lord, stoned to death (Josephus, *Antiquities,* 20:9.1).

63	-Paul is set free, and possibly goes to Spain.
64	-1 Peter and the Gospel of Mark.
65	-Paul at Ephesus, Crete, and Macedonia. 1st Letter to Timothy, probably Titus.
66-67	-Jewish revolt. Josephus is taken prisoner.
	-Martyrdom of Peter and Paul in Rome
68	-Nero commits suicide.
70	-Jerusalem and the Temple are totally destroyed by Roman Legions to end the Jewish revolt.
70-80	-Letter of Jude, 2 Peter. The Greek Gospel of Matthew, Gospel of Luke, Acts of the Apostles.
93	-*The Antiquities of the Jews* by Josephus.
95	-John exiled to Patmos. Final text of Revelation. 1 John (3 John and 2 John are possibly earlier). Death of

The Historical Perspective

John at Ephesus.

132-135   -Second Jewish rebellion. Jerusalem be-
           comes a Roman colony, forbidden to the
           Jews.

306   -Constantine becomes a Roman Co-
           Emperor.

313   -Edict of Milan by Constantine restores
           Christian property and grants further
           freedoms.

380   -Christianity declared to be the official
           religion of the Roman Empire.

CHAPTER 1

Jesus and His Family

1. THE EARLY YEARS OF JESUS

The New Testament tells us about the birth of Jesus at Bethlehem and his family's return to Nazareth after a brief exile in Egypt to avoid death at the hands of Herod the Great. Luke tells us that at Nazareth "the child grew to maturity, and he was filled with wisdom; and God's favor was with him (2:40). Next, we find that he went with his family to Jerusalem for the Passover when he was 12 years old, and there he discussed Scripture with the doctors. After that, Jesus returned with his family to Nazareth and increased in wisdom and "stature" (Luke 2:52). Nothing else is said about his childhood or circumstances at Nazareth until he is again introduced to us by John the Baptist and begins his mission.

But he must have been active in the synagogue and village life at Nazareth. From Matthew 13:55 we learn that the citizens of Nazareth, whom he taught in their synagogue, were astonished at the wisdom he displayed, since he was of humble origin, "the carpenter's son."

The family house probably consisted of one or two rooms, possibly three, with the tools of the family trade mingled with simple home furnishings. As in all Jewish families, religion must have been paramount in that home. A Jewish father's most sacred duty was to teach his child the religion of his people (Deut. 6:4-9). While the Temple at Jerusalem was the center of religious life in the Nazareth home of Jesus (Luke 2:41, "Every year his parents used to go to Jerusalem for the feast of the Passover"), we know from Matthew 13:53-54 that Nazareth also had a viable synagogue.

And it was the synagogue where worship and instruction in religion were cultivated. It was there that Jesus would have heard scripture in Hebrew every week, followed by translation into Aramaic, the common language of Judea, and instruction for daily life. From the age of about six years on, Jesus would have been taught the scriptures, which was the customary Jewish practice, facts which seem to be confirmed by the gospels (Luke 4:16-17). Since schools under the control of the synagogue had been established in most towns during that time, it is safe to assume that Jesus received a comprehensive religious education at home, in the synagogue, and at such schools, as anything less would have been completely contrary to Jewish customs. From the New Testament, however, we know nothing about his education, other than that he grew in "wisdom and in favor with God and man" (Luke 2:52), which, coupled with those Jewish customs of religious education of the time, should be more than sufficient refutation of the claim by the Quest for the Historical Jesus scholars of today that he was an illiterate Jewish peasant of a landless class.

JESUS OF NAZARETH

Although it is clear that Jesus and his family were not peasants, but residents of the town of Nazareth in which the family carried on the trade of carpentry, it is also apparent that Jesus was in tune with nature, as the parables and other teachings of Jesus reveal an intimate familiarity with the world of nature. One can well imagine that he spent hours wandering the fields and hills around Nazareth during his formative teenage years. What he saw then is best stated by Ernest Renan, a French expert on Middle East ancient languages and civilizations, philosopher and writer, whose popular *Life of Jesus* (*Vie de Jésus*), published in 1863, is extensively treated by Albert Schweitzer in his monumental work *The Quest of the Historical Jesus*. Renan had visited Nazareth, which at that time was little changed from the time of Jesus. His description of what Jesus probably saw on his solitary walks is: "The view from the town is limited; but if we ascend a little to the plateau swept by a perpetual breeze, which stands above the highest houses, the landscape is magnificent. On the west stretch the fine outlines of Carmel, terminating in an abrupt spur which seems to run down sheer to the sea. Next, one sees the double summit which towers above Megiddo; the mountains of the country of Shechem, with their holy places of the patriarchal period; the hills of *Gilboa, the small picturesque group to which is attached the graceful or terrible recollections of Shunem and of Endor; and Tabor, with its beautiful rounded form, which antiquity compared to a bosom. Through a gap between the mountains of Shunem and Tabor are visible the valley of the Jordan and the high plains of Perea, which form a continuous line from the eastern side. On the north, the mountains of Safed, stretching towards the sea, conceal St. Jean d'Acre, but leave the Gulf of Khaifa in sight. Such was the horizon, of Jesus. This enchanted circle, cradle of the kingdom of God, was for years his world. Indeed, during his whole life he went but little beyond the familiar bounds of his childhood. For yonder, northwards, one can almost see, on the flank of Hermon, Cæsarea-Philippi, his farthest point of advance into the Gentile world; and to the south the less smiling aspect of these Samaritan hills foreshadows the dreariness of Judea beyond, parched as by a burning wind of desolation and death."

[Note: In 1 Samuel 28:4-25, Saul consulted the Witch of Endor on the evening before the Battle of Gilboa, where Saul fought the Philistines who had pitched camp at Shunem. King Saul perished in that battle as prophesized by Samuel, whom the witch had conjured up from the dead. Saul was the first king of the United Kingdom of Israel and reigned 1049 –1007 BC. David, who had triumphed over Goliath, succeeded to the throne.]

2. HIS BROTHERS

Without any qualification, the gospels tell us that Jesus had brothers and sisters. In Matthew 12:46-45 we read that his mother and his brothers appeared while he was speaking to the crowds. They were standing apart from the crowd and anxious to talk with him. In another reference to his family, Matthew 13:55-56 recites the astonishment of those members of the synagogue at Nazareth where he taught. They wondered where he got his wisdom and his miraculous powers. "Is not his mother the woman called Mary?" they asked. "And his brothers James and Joseph and Simon and Jude? His sisters too, are they not all here with us?" This scene is substantially repeated in Mark 6:3-4.

We also know that after the crucifixion, his brothers James and Jude were active as leaders in the Church. And from the gospel of John, we learn that even before that his brothers were listening to Jesus and were possibly participants in his mission. His brothers were with him during the time of his mission in Galilee, but perhaps not entirely convinced of his divinity.

"After this, Jesus went around in Galilee. He did not want to go about in Judea because the Jewish leaders there were looking for a way to kill him. But when the Jewish Festival of Tabernacles was near, Jesus' brothers said to him, 'Leave Galilee and go to Judea, so that your disciples there may see the works you do. No one who wants to become a public figure acts in secret. Since you are doing these things, show yourself to the world.' For even his own brothers did not believe in him. Therefore Jesus told them, 'My time is not yet here; for you any time will do. The

The Historical Perspective

*world cannot hate you, but it hates me because I tes-
tify that its works are evil. You go to the festival. I am
not going up to this festival, because my time has not
yet fully come.' After he had said this, he stayed in
Galilee. However, after his brothers had left for the
festival, he went also, not publicly, but in secret"* (Bible, NIV, pp. 972-973, John 7:1-6).

And in Galatians 1:20, Paul refers to James as
the brother of the Lord.

Nevertheless, *The Jerusalem Bible,* prepared by a
collaboration of Catholic translators at Christ's College, Liverpool, states that they were "not Mary's
children but near relations, cousins perhaps, which
both Hebrew and Aramaic style 'brothers'." Several
sections of Scripture are then cited to support that
proposition. It seems, however, that in these scriptures, members of the same religion, cult, or tribe
were considered "brothers," which is not at all a
strange interpretation when we recognize that English is frequently used in the same context today.

We find in Paul further evidence that they were
not cousins when he makes a clear reference to the
brothers of Jesus, as distinct from the Apostles. In 1
Corinthians 9:5, Paul says: "Don't we have the right
to take a believing wife along with us, as do the other
apostles and the Lord's brothers and Cephas
(Peter)?"

It stretches the imagination to claim that the
plain and ordinary language of Matthew, which
states that our Lord had brothers and sisters, actu-

ally means that he had cousins or other distant relatives.

When we go outside the biblical texts, we find that Josephus, the Jewish historian, states unequivocally that James was the brother of Jesus. The Roman governor had died, and while his replacement was still on his way to Judea, the Jewish King Agrippa appointed Ananias, of the sect of the Sadducees, to the office of high priest. The new high priest quickly assembled the Sanhedrin, and brought before them "the brother of Jesus, who was called the Christ, whose name was James and some others; and when he had formed an accusation against them as breakers of the law, he delivered them to be stoned."

Dr. Paul L. Maier notes in his *Josephus, The Essential Works,* p. 285, that the New Testament could not have been Josephus' source for this account of the death of James, because the New Testament provides no details on James' death.

We can make two important observations from this report by Josephus. First, we know from Josephus, a non-Christian historian of great repute, that James, the brother of Jesus, was stoned after a short trial before the Sanhedrin. This may well be some of the best non-biblical evidence of the divinity of Jesus, because, if Jesus were a hoax or fraud, who would know that better than his brother, James. If James was willing to stand up for Jesus before the Sanhedrin, and then accept execution by stoning, when he could have stopped the proceedings at any time by recanting and pleading for mercy, that is good evidence of the true nature of Jesus and the firm belief of James. Next, Josephus does not refer to "the others" who were brought before the Sanhedrin with James as brothers of Jesus.

Clearly, then, Josephus, who had all the facts at hand and was living in Jerusalem at the time, meant that James was the brother of Jesus as the term is understood in plain and simple everyday language.

The real question is whether these brothers and sisters were children of Joseph prior to his engagement to Mary, or younger siblings of Jesus. An argument can be made in support of each proposition.

The Argument in Favor of Older Siblings

Prior to the 4th century, it was commonly understood that Jesus' "brothers" were older sons of Joseph though not of Mary. According to early Christian tradition (oral or written beliefs which are not part of the Bible) Joseph was a widower with children at the time he married. Eusebius, a respected early Church historian, wrote around the year 300 AD that, "James was called the brother of the Lord because he was a son of Joseph."

The earliest surviving record prior to Eusebius is the *Protoevangelium of James*, also known as the Gospel of James. A copy first appeared around 120 AD. This document states that Joseph was a widower who already had a family. It is the oldest source to assert the virginity of Mary after the birth of Jesus. The document claims to be written by

James, the brother of Jesus, and in the text he claims he is the son of Joseph from a prior marriage. However, the document has not generally been accepted as authentic, although it may be the source used by Eusebius.

Many scholars give considerable weight to the early tradition that the brothers were sons of Joseph from a prior marriage, as there must have been many things known to the early Christians concerning the life of Jesus, and passed down from generation to generation, and nothing outside the Scriptures has been found or discovered to conclusively suggest otherwise.

The next question faced by proponents of older siblings is: "Where were they when Joseph and Mary went to Bethlehem?" That question suggests they were born later. But, it is also possible that they were old enough to be left behind under the protection of other family members to be registered in Nazareth. It may have been Mary who desired that Jesus be registered in Bethlehem since she was also of the House of David.

The overall impression should control. It seems they were older and concerned when they went looking for Jesus with Mary, as Matthew reported. Others may have a different view, and conclude they were younger children of Mary and Joseph, a suggestion close to blasphemy for many Christians.

Perhaps James was as much as twenty years older, for he appears to be an authoritative figure and a spokesman for Jesus after his crucifixion. It seems less likely that the word of James would have been so readily accepted if he were a younger brother of Jesus.

The passage in John 7, above, could be the best evidence that Jesus' brothers were older. In Jewish families, the eldest brother was venerated on a level with the father. After the death of the father, he became the head of the family. Most scholars believe that Joseph died long before Jesus started on his mission. If Jesus were the older brother and head of the family, one can not imagine his younger brothers taunting him by saying, "No one who wants to become a public figure acts in secret. Since you are doing these things, show yourself to the world."

It is generally accepted that James, the "brother of the Lord," led the Christian community in Jerusalem and authored *The Letter of James*, written in Greek about the year 45 AD. Addressed to the Jewish Christians scattered throughout the world, it is skillfully written in Greek. And this letter, written before any of the gospels, was accepted from the very beginning, since James, although not one of the Twelve, as the brother of Jesus was a recognized apostolic authority. This is a good argument for an older, seasoned man.

James' eloquence in Greek is also further evidence that Jesus, as a man, was no ordinary man, nor did he come from an ordinary peasant family, but a family that had close ties to the synagogue at Nazareth, was familiar with the Scriptures, and also fluent in Greek, the international language of politics and commerce.

A second brother, Jude, who refers to himself as "brother of James," is identified as one of the "brothers of the Lord" in Matthew 13:55. In *The Letter of Jude*, probably written after the stoning of James, Jude also writes proficiently in Greek, which is good evidence that this family was not illiterate peasant stock, as is claimed by "scholars" of the current "Quest for the Historical Jesus" movement, discussed later.

Finally, the claims of early Christian tradition that they were older brothers of Jesus developed while James served as the leader of the Church and Jude was active in its mission. This leaves little room for further argument, especially without proof to the contrary.

The Argument in Favor of Younger Siblings

There is no compelling reason to believe that Mary could not have had other children, other than the claim that Mary was a perpetual virgin. This doctrine developed later in Catholic theology, and offers no proof in Scripture. On the contrary, one reference in the Bible could lead to the opposite conclusion. At the crucifixion, Matthew 27:55-56 states that "Many women were there, watching from a distance. They had followed Jesus from Galilee to care for his needs. Among them were Mary Magdalene, Mary the mother of James and Joseph, and the mother of Zebedee's sons."

The Historical Perspective

Remembering that Matthew 13:55 reported, "Isn't his mother's name Mary, and aren't his brothers James, Joseph, Simon and Judas?" one can claim that this Mary, at the cross with Mary Magdalene, is the mother of Jesus. And not only is she the mother of Jesus, this is clear evidence that she was also the mother of James and Joseph, referred to as brothers of Jesus in Matthew 13. That being the case, one wonders why this passage does not identify her as the mother of Jesus. But when we look to Mark at 15:40, he describes the women on Calvary with one important distinction: "Among them were Mary of Magdala, Mary who was the mother of James the younger (not James the brother of the Lord) and Joseph, and Salome."

Further argument against Mary as the mother of James and Joseph is that "Mary," described as the mother of James and Joseph in Matthew, could well be Mary the wife of Clopas. John 19:25 states, "Near the cross of Jesus stood his mother, his mother's sister, Mary the wife of Clopas, and Mary Magdalene."

The next sentence in John raises another question. If James and Joseph are younger brothers of Jesus, why didn't Jesus leave Mary to their care, rather than John? "When Jesus saw his mother there, and the disciple whom he loved standing nearby, he said to her, 'Woman, here is your son,' and to the disciple, 'Here is your mother.' From that time on, this disciple took her into his home" (John 19:26-27). The answer to that question could be that the brothers were much younger.

Although we can not accept Matthew and Mark as authority for the proposition that the mother of James and Joseph at the cross is Mary, the mother of Jesus, we still have the earlier references to his mother appearing with his brothers, James, Joseph, Simeon and Jude, who appear to be younger brothers, rather than older sons of Joseph, who likely would have been married and living apart at the time.

Thus, James, as a younger brother of the Lord, who wrote the *Letter of James* in AD 45, could have been between 45 and 50 years of age at the time, which accounts for the maturity of that epistle. Were he a much older brother, old enough to have been left behind during the journey to Bethlehem, he would have been around 65 to 70 years of age at that time, and around 85 to 90 when he was stoned to death in the year AD 62, which is unlikely.

The same can be said of Jude. His letter was written around 70-80 AD, which would make him 90-100 years of age, also unlikely. The more likely case seems to suggest that he was a younger brother and not more than 70-80 years old when he wrote his epistle, which is, again, a well-seasoned age.

Returning to the earlier references to the brothers of Jesus, we find that John tells us that the first sign given by Jesus was at the wedding at Cana in Galilee, when he turned water into wine, and that "After this he went down to Capernaum with his mother and brothers and his disciples" (John 2:12, NIV). Since this is the beginning of his mission, it is more probable that these brothers were younger brothers, and not older half-brothers, who would have no reason to accompany him at that point. This is especially true since Paul, as stated above, tells us that the brothers of Jesus were married, and as older brothers, they would have been well past the age of marriage at this time ("Don't we have the right to take a believing wife along with us, as do the other apostles and the Lord's brothers and Cephas?" 1 Corinthians 9:5).

However, *The Jerusalem Bible* translates this passage from John as: "After this, he went down to Capernaum with his mother and the brothers." And in the footnote to that passage, *The Jerusalem Bible* states that the brothers are not blood-brothers of Jesus, but the inner circle of his first disciples. A rebuttal of that statement would suggest there was no inner-circle of disciples at that time, other than the disciples already mentioned in the NIV version, which declares that both his disciples and his brothers went to Capernaum with him, and his mother and Peter.

Examining again Matthew 12:46-47, which states, "While Jesus was still talking to the crowd, his mother and brothers stood outside, wanting to speak to him," it is just as unlikely that these siblings were older half-brothers as it is unlikely they were cousins. Jesus was at least thirty years old. Why would older half-brothers be checking up on him? Isn't it more likely they were younger brothers, possibly even teenagers, which is why they were with Mary and why they were not old enough to be given the care of Mary at Calvary?

In conclusion, relying strictly upon Scripture; the weight of evidence suggests the brothers were younger. On the other hand, early Church leaders and historians were closer to the time and knew much about Jesus; therefore, the claim that the brothers were sons of Joseph by a prior marriage can not be completely discounted. Yet, in the final analysis, it really makes little difference whether they were older or younger.

3. JOHN THE BAPTIST

John the Baptist is described as a relative of Jesus in the Gospel of Luke, when the angel tells Mary that her kinswoman, Elizabeth, had in her old age, also conceived a son (1:36-37). Mary visited Elizabeth in a town in Judah, commonly identified as Ain Karim, about 5 miles West of Jerusalem, and Elizabeth received her as "the mother of my Lord." If Mary were a resident of Nazareth or Sepphoris (possibly the home of her parents) the journey to visit Elizabeth would have taken a few days. Assuming Mary's parents were devout Jews, it is also probable that the family was visiting the Temple at Jerusalem, in which case Ain Karim would have been a little over an hour's walk. It is interesting to note that Luke does not identify Mary and Elizabeth as "sisters," which is possibly further evidence that the brothers of Jesus were brothers, and not merely kin.

40

The Historical Perspective

There is no mention of a family relationship between John the Baptist, son of Elizabeth, and Jesus, in the other gospels.

Matthew, the first gospel to be written, after relating the ancestry of Jesus, his birth in Bethlehem, and events leading to Nazareth, simply introduces John the Baptist with the statement: "In due course, John the Baptist appeared" (3:1). "Then Jesus appeared, he came from Galilee to the Jordan to be baptized by John" (3:13).

Mark, the second gospel, begins with the preaching of John the Baptist and omits entirely any account of the birth of Jesus or his early years, and says: "It was at this time that Jesus came from Nazareth in Galilee and was baptized in the Jordan by John" (1:9).

The fourth gospel, John, begins with the theological statement that Jesus always existed, he was the Word, and was with God from the beginning. John (the Baptist) was sent by God in advance to be a witness to the coming of Jesus, "and the Word was made flesh and lived among us" (1:1-14). John also omits entirely any reference to a birth at Bethlehem or any mention of Jesus until his baptism by John in the Jordan. Thus, both Mark and John began their accounts with the beginning of the ministry of Jesus, while Matthew and Luke include the birth of Jesus and the biographical material leading up to that time. Since only Luke makes the claim that John and Jesus were cousins, many scholars discount that statement.

JESUS OF NAZARETH

However, as is the case with Jesus, there can be no argument that John the Baptist actually lived. Again, we can look to the Jewish historian Josephus for an account of his execution. In *Antiquities*, 18:5, Josephus states that: Herod (Antipas) had lost a battle with his father-in-law, and that some of the Jews thought that his defeat came from God as punishment for what he had done to John, "that was called the Baptist." Josephus does not mention Salome and her dance (Matthew 14:3-12; Mark 6:17-29) as the reason for the execution, but gives the more probable explanation, being that Herod was fearful of the "great influence John had over the people" and that a rebellion could easily come about because they seemed "ready to do anything he should advise." Herod "thought it best, by putting him to death, to prevent any mischief he might cause." Therefore, he had him taken prisoner to the fortress at Macherus, "and was there put to death." Josephus describes John the Baptist as a good man, who commanded the Jews to exercise virtue, to be pious, and exercise righteousness towards one another, and that John called for baptism for purification of the body, and not the remission of sin, as the soul was to be thoroughly purified beforehand through righteousness. Josephus concludes his account of the execution of John the Baptist by saying: "Now the Jews had an opinion that the destruction of this army was sent as punishment upon Herod, and a mark of God's displeasure to him."

In the New Testament accounts of the death of

The Historical Perspective

John the Baptist, Herod had John imprisoned for denouncing his marriage, and John was later executed by beheading. John had condemned Herod for marrying Herodias, the wife of his brother Philip, in violation of Old Testament Law. Later, the daughter of Herodias danced before Herod, who offered the daughter a favor in return. The mother, Herodias, told her to ask for the head of John the Baptist, which was delivered to her on a plate (Mark 6:14-29). It is possible that both accounts are true.

It is also interesting to note that the Gospels of Matthew and Mark do not mention the name Salome, but only describe her as the daughter of Herodias who came in and danced. How the name Salome became popular in Christian tradition is somewhat of a mystery. Josephus states further in Chapter 5 of Book 18 of his *Jewish Antiquities* that Herodias had a daughter named Salome, and that after her birth Herodias divorced her husband and married Herod [Antipas], her former husband's brother (both sons of Herod the Great). Thus, it appears that the accounts which name the daughter as Salome and as the step-daughter of Herod, are correct. Josephus does not, however, give Salome as the reason for John's beheading. Salome is listed by him merely as part of a detailed account of the descendants of Herod the Great.

CHAPTER 2

The Historical Records

The first question many ask regarding the life of Jesus of Nazareth is: "Do you mean he actually existed?" The answer is: "Of course he did." The historical record establishes beyond a doubt that Jesus lived in Galilee and that he was crucified in Jerusalem by Pontius Pilate.

However, the popular notion seems to be that Jesus is a creature of fiction. That concept of Jesus has made its way into such films as *Religulous* and *The God Who Wasn't There*, a 2005 independent documentary which questions the existence of Jesus and purportedly examines the evidence supporting the "Christ as myth" theory against the evidence of a historical Jesus. This position is supported by a few modern writers who claim that attempts to use the gospels to reconstruct the life of Jesus gives too much credit to the New Testament accounts, and that it is more likely that Jesus never existed. The well known philosopher Bertrand Russell also doubted the existence of Jesus. Others argue that Jesus is a fictional character derived from pagan gods such as Dionysus. However, the "fictional Jesus" theory is not held by the great majority of professional historians or New Testament scholars. And now the pendulum appears to be swinging the other way. The question has become why should we so completely

The Historical Perspective

disregard the accounts of a "Jesus of Nazareth who was crucified by Pontius Pilate" written by recognized historians of that time?

The best contemporary source of information regarding Jesus of Nazareth is the Jewish historian Josephus (a non-Christian), who was born about four years after the crucifixion in 37 AD, and died right at the turn of the first century in 100 AD. Josephus came from the upper classes of Jewish society and was, perhaps, the most respected historian of that era.

"He was the most famous Jew of his time not only among his fellow countrymen, but among the Romans also, so that he was honored with a statute erected in the city of Rome and the inclusion of his works in its library" (Eusebius. *The Church History*, translation and commentary by Dr. Paul L. Maier, Kregel Publications 1999, 2007)

Josephus wrote a comprehensive history of the Jews under the title of *Antiquities of the Jews.* In an early manuscript of that book, Josephus, states that: "At this time there was a wise man called Jesus, and his conduct was good, and he was known to be virtuous. Many people among the Jews and the other nations became his disciples. Pilate condemned him to be crucified and to die. But those who had become his disciples did not abandon his discipleship. They reported that he had appeared to them three days after his crucifixion and that he was alive...." Although there is some controversy concerning exactly what else Josephus said concerning Jesus, this report of the crucifixion under Pontius Pilate is generally accepted as authentic.

Josephus again mentions Jesus when telling about the martyrdom of James, the "brother of Jesus, who is called the Christ" (*Antiquities,* 20:9.1).

And when reporting on John the Baptist, Josephus goes into great detail (*Antiquities,* 28:5.2).

Tacitus (56 – 117 AD, a senator and a historian of the Roman Empire) reported that the Christians "derived their name and origin from one Christ, who in the reign of Tiberius had suffered death by the sentence of the prefect, Pontius Pilate" (Annals, xv. 44).

Suetonius (69-140 AD, another Roman historian) in writing his *Lives of the twelve Caesars,* makes an obscure allusion to Christ as the reason he assigns for the edict of Claudius expelling the Jews from Rome (Vit. Claud. 25).

The younger Pliny (61-112 AD) reported that the Christian community in Bithynia was accustomed to honor Christ as God (Epistles X. 96). This epistle is a report by Pliny from Bithynia about the year 103 AD to the Roman emperor on his actions against the followers of Christ. He asked the emperor for instructions on dealing with Christians, and explained that he forced Christians to curse Christ under painful torture. Pliny states further in his report that: "In the meanwhile, the method I have observed towards those ... Christians is this: I interrogated them whether they were Christians; if they confessed it [maintained their faith] I repeated the question twice again, adding the threat of capital punishment; if they still persevered, I ordered them to be executed."

Regarding Pontius Pilate, the above sources confirm that he actually existed and was the Roman governor of Judea during the life of Jesus. According to Josephus, Pilate was finally ordered back to Rome in the year 36 AD at the end of a ten-year term after harshly suppressing a Samaritan uprising, arriving back in Rome just after the death of the Roman emperor Tiberius (*Antiquities,* 18:89) which occurred on March 16 in the year 37 AD.

Archaeological findings further confirm Pontius Pilate as a prefect of Roman-controlled Judea. In 1961 a limestone block was discovered by Italian archaeologists while excavating an ancient theater in the city of Caesarea, which was the capital of Judea at the time Pontius Pilate was governor. A partially damaged inscription on the block, as reconstructed and translated into English reads: *Pontius Pilate, Prefect of Judea, has dedicated this Tiberieum to the Caesareans.* The exact meaning of the word "Tiberieum" is not known, and some scholars have speculated that it was some type of structure built in dedication to the emperor Tiberius. Apparently, that structure was demolished or fell into disrepair, and the stone was used again later in the construction of a theater.

Finally, there are four history books covering the life of Jesus. These are the Gospels of Matthew, Mark, Luke and John. Without regard to Christian theology or the authenticity of the miracles claimed to have been performed by Jesus, one simply cannot disregard the narrative of events and the descriptions of people involved in the life of Jesus, because many of the events described and the important persons of the era can and have been independently verified by non-Biblical sources.

Matthew, the tax-collector, was one of the Apostles, and was the first to write. He wrote his gospel in the common Aramaic language for Jews who had converted to Christianity. His gospel was then translated into Greek, the literary and international language of the time. Mark, a disciple from Jerusalem who assisted Paul in his missionary work, and later Peter, who's interpreter he was, wrote down Peter's preaching in Rome. Another disciple, Luke, a medical man born at Antioch, and probably not Jewish, accompanied Paul on his second and third missions and was with him during his two Roman captivities, for which reason his gospel could claim the authority of Paul. Luke also wrote the "Acts of the Apostles," which is the first history of the rise of Christianity. Both Mark and Luke wrote in Greek. The fourth gospel, John, also written in Greek, was likely written in large part by John the Apostle, and is more concerned with the significance of the events in Christ's life and what he did and said.

Those who still may have some doubts as to whether Jesus of Nazareth existed, or whether the New Testament contains a factual portrayal of his life and the early Church, should stop at this point

The Historical Perspective

and read *In the Fullness of Time,* A Historian Looks at Christmas, Easter, and the Early Church, by Paul L. Maier, Kregel Publications, 1997, ISBN 978-0-8254-3329-0.

CHAPTER 3

The Elusive Date

We all love certainty. But there is nothing certain about the date for Jesus' birth. However, the uncertainty is not as unusual as one might first think. Martin Luther knew the day of the year he was born, because he was born the day before St. Martin's day, the day on which he was baptized. But he was off on his age. His close associate, Philip Melanchton, felt compelled to tell him, "You know, Martin, your mother says you are a year older." And many Russian Jews who immigrated to America after the Second World War were not sure of their age or the year they were born within two or three years.

Our calendar, based upon the year 1 AD for the birth of Christ was not developed until the 6th Century. Before that time, the Romans used a calendar based upon the founding of the City of Rome for many historical events, while reporting other events as having occurred during the reign of a certain emperor, such as the 15th year of the reign of the Emperor Tiberius, etc. In the area now known as Palestine, which was largely Galilee, Samaria and Judea during the life of Jesus, there was no common calendar. Nor were records of births recorded in any official documents.

For almost 2000 years, Church tradition and the Julian calendar insisted that Jesus was born in the

The Historical Perspective

year 01 AD (year of our Lord). Many modern Bibles, including study bibles, still insist on a chronology beginning with the year 01 AD for the birth of Jesus and ending with the crucifixion during the year 33 AD, when Jesus was 33 years of age.

In the year now known as 525 AD the monk Dionysius invented the Anno Domini era, or Julian, calendar, which is used as the basis for the Gregorian calendar of today. Dionysius used his new calendar for his Easter Table, but he did not use it to date any historical event. He himself stated that the "present year" was "the consulship of Probus Junior", which he stated was 525 years "since the incarnation of our Lord Jesus Christ." No one knows exactly how he arrived at that number. But it was obviously wrong, because we know that Jesus was born during the reign of Herod the Great, who died four years before the year Dionysius gave us for the birth of Jesus.

The writers of our gospels referred to the terms of certain rulers to date events. When reporting on the life of Jesus, the gospels are the most accurate historical books we have. And there is no reason to be bashful about accepting what the gospels tell us are "the facts," no matter what might be politically correct or accepted Church tradition today. Luke, the physician, was the most precise of the gospel writers. And it all probably began with him.

In reading Luke, the monk Dionysius noted that in Luke 3:1-3, he tells us very precisely that John the Baptist began teaching in the fifteenth year of Tiberius Caesar's reign, when Pontius Pilate was governor of Judea, Herod (Antipas) was tetrarch (a title for Roman puppet ruler) of Galilee, his brother Philip was tetrarch of the lands of Ituraea and Trachonitis, and Lysanias was tetrarch of Abilene, all during the pontificate of Annas and Caiaphas (high priests).

Dionysius knew when Tiberius became emperor according to the Roman calendar, which is based upon the founding of Rome as year one. Dionysius also knew from the gospels that Jesus was about 30 years old when he began his mission. Therefore, Jesus was 29 during the 15th year of the reign of Tiberius, when John the Baptist began teaching, Jesus was 30 when he began his mission early the following year, and 33 when he was crucified after a mission lasting a little over three years. Although at first reading, Luke seems to report that the ministry of Jesus lasted only one year, we learn from John that the ministry of Jesus covered a period of a little over three years. The explanation is that while Luke, as well as Matthew and Mark, give the appearance of having bundled all of the events reported as having occurred during one year, these authors actually made no attempt to report events as having occurred in any particular year at all. And, although the events are presented in chronological order for the most part, Matthew, Mark and Luke were more interested in reporting what Jesus did and said and the importance of his message, rather than when he did or said anything in particular.

Therefore, it appears that Dionysius probably developed his calendar by using the year 33 AD for the crucifixion, and then worked backward 33 years for the date of Christ's birth. Thus, the year 753 on the Roman calendar became the year 1 AD in the new calendar developed by Dionysius. But Herod the Great had died in the Roman year of 749, four years before that. Using the new calendar developed by Dionysius, this means that Herod the Great died in the year 4 BC, or four years before the birth of Christ. Apparently, Dionysius failed to read the gospels more carefully.

Luke tells us that at the time of the birth of Christ, Caesar Augustus decreed that a census of the Roman world population be taken, and this first census took place while Quirinius was governor of Syria. Therefore, Joseph set out from Nazareth with Mary to be registered at Bethlehem as being of the House of David. Matthew tells us that Jesus was born at Bethlehem in Judea during the reign of King Herod. King Herod died in early 04 BC, so we know Jesus was born before that. From Egyptian sources, we know there was a census in 08 BC, and Quirinius was appointed by Rome to carry out the census, although he did not become governor of Syria until later. For confirmation, we have the statement of Tertullian (an independent source) that a census had been taken in Judea under Augustus about 9 to 7 BC. The Edict of 08 BC, ordering that census, would have been carried out the following years, being 07 and 06 BC, and that was probably when Jesus was born. The only mistake Luke may have made is that he did not realize Quirinius was not yet governor of Syria when he was appointed by Rome to carry out the census. Quirinius did become governor of Syria later.

The statement of Tertullian (Against Marcion, iv. 19) that a census had been taken in Judea under Augustus by Sentius Saturninus, who was the governor of Syria about 9 to 7 BC, certainly comes from some source independent of the gospels, and tends to confirm Luke's account of a census before the death of Herod. Tertullian (c. 160 – c. 220 AD) was a prolific early Christian author from Carthage.

Footnote b to Luke 2:1-2 in the *Jerusalem Bible* , a collaboration of Christ's College, Liverpool, England, published in 1966 with the Imprimatur of the Catholic Church states that: "The most probable explanation is that the census, which was made with a view to taxation, took place about 8-6 BC, and if so Luke's expression would then be a rough approximation. Jesus was born certainly before Herod's death (4 BC), possibly in 8-6 BC. The 'Christian era', established by Dionysius in the 6th century is the result of a false calculation." Without further explanation, *The Jerusalem Bible* then dates the beginning of Jesus' ministry in the autumn of 27 AD, with his crucifixion taking place in the year 30 AD.

Other respected scholars have arrived at yet different dates. The historian Paul L. Maier places the crucifixion during the year 33 AD and the birth of Christ during the fall or winter of 5 BC. Benjamin Rush Rhees, discussed more thoroughly later, gives the year 6 BC as a probable date for the birth of Jesus and states that Jesus was likely baptized in 26 AD and crucified in the year 30 AD. No one who has studied the problem, however, places the birth of Jesus during the year 1 AD, as determined by the monk Dionysius.

The account given in Matthew of "the star" which drew the wise men to Judea gives no sure help in determining the date of the birth of Jesus, but it is at least suggestive that in the spring and autumn of BC 7 there occurred a remarkable conjunction of the planets Jupiter and Saturn. This was first noticed by Kepler in consequence of a similar conjunction observed by him in AD 1603. Men much influenced by astrology must have been impressed by such a celestial phenomenon, but whether it furnishes an explanation for the star of the wise men is not clear. If it does, it confirms the date otherwise probable for the nativity, that is, not far from BC 6. It therefore seems probable that Jesus was born in the summer of BC 7 or 6.

Although there remains some speculation as to the exact date for the birth of Jesus and the beginning of his ministry according to our calendar, Luke had no such difficulties. And if one wonders what could be the source for the information reported by Luke and others in the gospels regarding the birth of Jesus, we need look no farther than Jesus' family. Mary, the mother of Jesus, certainly knew when he was born, as did James and the other older brothers of Jesus. Mary, as well as the brothers James and

Jude, and possibly other siblings would have been available for reference at the time of the oral traditions upon which the gospels were based, and even at the time they were written down.

There are some things we do know for certain. From other, non-Biblical sources, we know that Jesus was crucified during the time Pontius Pilate was governor of Judea, and that Pilate was governor during the period 26-36 AD. And although the gospels indicate that Jesus was about thirty years old when he began his mission, he may have been older than that by as much as 5-6 years, and his mission may well have lasted longer three years. When the Pharisees challenged Jesus at the Temple court, they said: "You are not yet fifty years old" (John 8:57), which indicates that he was older than thirty-three.

When one makes a careful study of the Gospel of John, it begins to make sense that it is very likely that Jesus' mission lasted much longer than three years for him to have accomplished all that is reported in that gospel. In any event, until more records are discovered or additional archeological findings are uncovered, we must be satisfied that this is all we can know concerning an exact date for the birth and death of Jesus. But it is clear that he did exist, even though we are unable to determine the date of his birth with any more certainly than others of that time period, such as Julius Caesar and Mark Antony and many other famous figures, all of whose dates of birth are subject to speculation and vary up to five or six years, depending upon the source.

CHAPTER 4

The World Background

In the year 143 BC Israel became an independent nation, shaking off centuries of occupation by one foreign power after another. This short period of freedom came to an end in 63 BC when the Jewish nation was conquered by the Roman General Pompey. Not until centuries later, was the nation of Israel to know freedom from foreign domination. However, subjugation by Rome was not as onerous as one might assume. Rome could be a benevolent master. The Roman policy was not to crush the peoples under Rome's control, but to give the populace as much autonomy as possible and the benefits of Roman civilization, even granting to some inhabitants the right of Roman citizenship and rapid advancement in the Roman army.

It was the beginning of the era known as the *Pax Romana*, a period of great peace and prosperity in the world under the protection of the Roman umbrella, a time when trade and commerce could flourish. Thus, although the Jews no longer enjoyed absolute freedom, Rome had brought to Israel an era of peace, prosperity, and a measure of freedom for the Jews, never again experienced. As Paul L. Maier points out *In the Fullness of Time,* it was also a time when a new religion springing to life in the ancient land of Israel could thrive and sweep rapidly throughout the known world

JESUS OF NAZARETH

But the *Pax Romana* had its growth pains. Pompey was not destined to remain in the world for long after conquering Jerusalem. Julius Caesar had completed his conquest of Gaul in 51 BC, extending Rome's territory to the English Channel and the Rhine, less than fifty years before Jesus was born. Following that, he built a bridge and crossed the Rhine, then invaded Britain. In 49 BC, Caesar marched back to Rome with his legions, and seized control of the government. He eventually met up with General Pompey and defeated him.

After five years in power as absolute dictator, Julius Caesar was assassinated by a group of senators led by Brutus. Mark Antony, a former staff officer in Julius Caesar's army and second in command at the time of Caesar's assassination, delivered the eulogy at Caesar's funeral, and resolved to avenge his murder. When Brutus and Cassius assembled an army to march on Rome, Antony, Octavian (later the Roman emperor Augustus) and Lepidus formed an alliance to stop the assassins. Brutus and Cassius were defeated. Octavian returned to Rome, Antony went on to govern the east, and Lepidus went on to govern Hispania and the province of Africa.

The father of Herod the Great, who had been put in power in Jerusalem by Pompey, made the mistake of supporting Brutus and the other assassins of Julius Caesar. However, Herod's father quickly switched his allegiance, and as a result was poisoned by supporters of the senate revolt against Julius Caesar. Herod executed his father's murderers, with

The Historical Perspective

Rome's blessing, and was rewarded with the office of puppet ruler in Jerusalem.

In the meantime Mark Antony had become involved in a quarrel with Octavian, so he summoned Cleopatra, the Queen of Egypt, to Tarsus, a city in south-central Turkey, and the birthplace of Saint Paul. Cleopatra reached the city in October, 41 BC. And notwithstanding the fact that Mark Antony was married to Octavian's sister, he and Cleopatra became lovers and formed an alliance. Antony then returned to Alexandria with her and spent the winter there. The following spring, Antony went to Rome and made peace with his brother-in-law, Octavian.

The Parthians (Persians), who had supported Brutus and Cassius in the civil war, showed further distain for the successors of Julius Caesar by invading Roman-controlled Syria, then promoted a revolt in Judea, kicked out Herod, and installed their own puppet king.

Herod fled to Rome for support, and was confirmed as king by the Roman Senate. However, because of rebellions in Sicily, the Romans were unable to furnish Antony with the necessary support to drive out the Persians and return Herod to power. Antony then sailed to Alexandria to obtain funding from Cleopatra, by then the mother of his twins. Cleopatra lent him the money he needed, and after capturing Jerusalem in 37 BC, Antony re-installed Herod as ruler, this time as "King" of Judaea, which included Galilee and Samaria.

Antony's further campaign against the Persians

ended in disaster and defeats. After another quarrel with Octavian, Antony again turned to Cleopatra for support, and successfully renewed his campaign against the Persians. In the meantime, Octavian dissolved the triumvirate with Antony and Lepidus, and assumed sole power. Antony was summoned to Rome, but remained in Alexandria with Cleopatra. Antony broke with Rome, and then distributed various former Roman lands under his control to his children as kingdoms, and proclaimed Cleopatra Queen of Queens and Queen of Egypt.

In 32 BC, the Senate deprived Antony of his powers and declared war against Cleopatra. Antony and Cleopatra's navy was destroyed at the battle of Actium off the coast of Greece, and they were forced to escape to Egypt. In August of 30 BC, Octavian invaded Egypt. Facing certain defeat, Antony and Cleopatra committed suicide, and Egypt became a Roman province.

Peace and prosperity followed, and in the year 23 BC the Roman puppet king, Herod, later known as Herod the Great, built a palace in Jerusalem. It was a fortified palace, built to protect the old city of Jerusalem, and consisted of two principal buildings, each with its own banquet halls, baths and accommodations for hundreds of guests. Pontius Pilate may have resided at this palace, during the time of Jesus' crucifixion, while Herod Antipas, the son of Herod the Great, probably resided at the Hasmonean palace halfway across Jerusalem toward the Temple.

Jesus was born during the last years of the reign

The Historical Perspective

of Herod the Great. Upon his death, Herod's kingdom was divided into three parts and distributed to his sons. However, Rome allowed none of his sons to take the title of king. The most able of Herod's sons was Philip, who ruled over the lands to the north and east of the Sea of Galilee. The other two brothers were Archelaus and Herod Antipas. Rome gave Archelaus control over Judea, Samaria, and Idumea. Herod Antipas was given the territory of Galilee and the land east of the Jordan and south of the Sea of Galilee, called Perea. Herod Antipas remained the ruler of Galilee all during the life of Jesus of Nazareth. He was a man of great passion and temper, and the one who executed John the Baptist. Although he had no authority in Jerusalem, he retained a palace in that city, where he often resided, especially during Passover, which is why he was there when Jesus was crucified. Since Herod Antipas was the ruler of Galilee, Pontius Pilate made an ineffective attempt to transfer jurisdiction of Jesus, a citizen of Galilee, to him. Referred to simply as Herod, Jesus described him as "that fox" (Luke 13:32). This was in response to a warning by some Pharisees who had come to tell Jesus that he should flee because Herod Antipas intended to kill him. Jesus replied that they should give that fox the message that today and tomorrow he would cast out devils, and on the third day he would attain his end, because it would not be right for a prophet to die outside Jerusalem.

Philip and Herod Antipas, remained in power un-

til after the death of Jesus. Philip died in AD 34, and
Antipas was deposed several years later, probably in
39 AD. The third brother, Archelaus ruled for a
much shorter time. He was deposed by Rome in AD
6, after being accused by the Jews of unbearable bar-
barity and tyranny. His brothers, Herod Antipas and
Philip had joined in that charge. The Gospel of Matthew would also seem to support the charge, as Joseph, when he learned that Archelaus had succeeded
his father as ruler of Judea, avoided that land on his
way back from Egypt to Galilee (Matthew 2:22).

After Archelaus was deposed, the areas he had
ruled as a puppet, Samaria, Judea and Jerusalem,
became an imperial province of Rome, governed by a
prefect appointed by the emperor from high-ranking
Roman citizens. The prefect was the representative
of the emperor in all areas of government. He commanded the auxiliary army, which, during the time
of Passover, when passions ran high in Jerusalem,
was brought in from Caesarea on the coast to beef up
the auxiliary troops stationed in the fortress north of
the Temple. The prefect was also the last and final
resort in all legal procedure, as well as the supervi-
sor for the collection of customs and taxes. In the
year AD 26, the Roman Emperor Tiberius sent Pontius Pilate to Judea as prefect. Pontius Pilate ruled
as the supreme Roman representative until AD 36,
when he was recalled to Rome to stand trial before
Tiberius on charges of cruelty and wanton killing of
Samaritans. His recall resulted from a complaint
lodged in Rome by the Samaritans, after his auxil-

The Historical Perspective

iary troops killed some of the innocent along with the probable culprits during a suspected religious uprising. In retrospect, his conduct at the trial of Jesus was disciplined and judicial in comparison with the many other recorded acts of Pontius Pilate. Fortunately for Pilate, Tiberius died before his trial.

Pontius Pilate may not have learned much from his recall, as Eusebius, an early Church historian, stated that Pilate suffered further misfortune in the reign of Caligula (AD 37–41), was exiled to Gaul and eventually committed suicide there in Vienne. The account of Eusebius is disputed by the historian Paul L. Maier in his notes to his novel *Pontius Pilate* and articles on the subject, in which Maier states that more likely Pontius Pilate lived out his life in peaceful retirement in Rome.

It was the fear of recall and trial at Rome, which finally induced Pilate to give Jesus over to be crucified, as Rome was ever cautious to appease the Jews to avoid open revolt, for which there was substantial justification by history. And in turn, the ruling Jews of the Sanhedrin were just as anxious to avoid any popular uprising, which would certainly result in a crushing retaliation by Roman legions, destruction of Jerusalem, and a thorough demolition of the Temple, the symbol of the Jewish nation. And that is exactly what the Romans did later in 70 AD, when a popular Jewish revolt could not be restrained, and the Roman army left not one stone of the city or Temple standing.

In this historical setting, there was little chance

that Jesus of Nazareth, who had earlier created a disturbance at the Temple by throwing out the money-changers, and now triumphantly entered the City of Jerusalem upon a donkey to the praise of the multitudes, would ever leave the city alive.

CHAPTER 5

Historical Notes of Interest

1. THE ROMAN ARMY

Rome maintained control through its legions. The bulk of the Roman army was stationed in Syria, just across the border to the north, and close enough to be brought in to suppress any revolt. Another contingent of Roman army auxiliary troops, composed primarily of men from the local populations was stationed in Caesarea on the coast, the home base of Pontius Pilate. During Passover, and other times when passions and rhetoric ran high, the troops were brought to Jerusalem and stationed in the barracks on the Temple Mount, to supplement the auxiliary troops in Jerusalem, and that is what Pontius Pilate had done at the time of Jesus' crucifixion. The auxiliary troops, quartered permanently in the barracks on the Temple Mount, were organized along the lines of the Roman army, but consisted primarily of Samaritans and other nationalities. All of the auxiliary troops, whether in Caesarea or Jerusalem, were under the control of the Roman Prefect. The officers, who could have been Roman citizens, were held to a higher standard, which is why the auxiliary officers were sent to Rome for trial after the revolt of 6 AD, while the troops were pardoned.

JESUS OF NAZARETH

In Galilee to the north and Perea across the Jordan, the soldiers were under the control of the Roman puppet, Herod Antipas, the son of Herod the Great, and were recruited from the local population and the Samaritans. The centurion of Capernaum (Mat. 8:5; Luke 7:2-5) was not an officer in the Roman army, but the army of Herod Antipas, who organized his army on the Roman pattern, with officers trained by the Imperial Roman forces.

The soldiers who beat and crucified Jesus were probably members of the auxiliary army brought to Jerusalem by Pontius Pilate during the Passover for two reasons: first, Jesus could not have been crucified by Temple guards acting under the orders of the Sanhedrin or high priest, because crucifixion was forbidden under Jewish law, and finally, the right of crucifixion was specifically reserved to the Romans.

2. TAXES

There were two types of Roman taxes in Judea at the time of Jesus, land and poll taxes, in the first category, and customs in the second category, with a different system of collecting each. In some cases there were other local taxes, such as occupation taxes, and church taxes. The Roman land taxes and poll taxes were collected by the Roman prefect, using salaried officials of the local Jewish courts. However, the contract for collecting Roman customs was awarded to the highest bidder. The work of collecting customs was then farmed out to representatives of those men who had bought the right to collect the dues assessed. The contractors, as well as their underlings are called publicans in the New Testament, although the name strictly applies only to the chief contractor. The tax collectors were despised because, in addition to their subservience to a hated foreign government, they had a reputation, usually deserved, for all sorts of extortion. In addition, they came from the most unscrupulous of the people. As is well known, the apostle Matthew had been a tax collector. He was the first to compose a gospel, being a continuous narrative of the deeds and words of Jesus covering his ministry on earth from baptism to resurrection.

3. EGYPT

For a fuller understanding of some passages of the New Testament, it is necessary to explore the situation in Egypt at the time of Jesus. And immediately, one finds a historical basis for early accounts in the gospels, namely, the flight to Egypt. After the birth of Jesus at Bethlehem and after the Magi had left, "an angel of the Lord appeared to Joseph in a dream. 'Get up,' he said, 'take the child and his mother and escape to Egypt. Stay there until I tell you, for Herod is going to search for the child to kill him'" (NIV, p. 876, Matthew 2:13). After a period of time, which could have been as much as two years or more, Joseph learned that Herod the Great was dead, and the family returned to Israel. "But when he heard that Archelaus was reigning in Judea in place of his father Herod (the Great), he was afraid to go there. Having been warned in a dream, he withdrew to the district of Galilee, and he went and lived in a town called Nazareth" (NIV, p. 876, Matthew 2:22). This passage from Matthew gives the impression that the family first moved to Nazareth after the birth of Jesus. However, Luke clarifies this point, and states that Joseph and Mary lived in Nazareth and had left from Nazareth to go to Bethlehem, and that they returned to Nazareth after Jesus was presented at the Temple, without mentioning the flight to Egypt.

Again, this is an example of discrepancies in the gospels, which probably result from a desire to emphasize other points, or because the information available to any particular author was not necessarily available to authors of the other gospels. But what is important in Matthew is his mention of Archelaus. And we know from non-biblical sources that Archelaus did rule in Judea after the death of his father, Herod the Great, and that his reign was so incompetent and brutal that he was removed from office by the Romans in 6 AD. Therefore, this incident is historically verified and it is entirely plausible that Joseph took a detour on his return to Galilee because of a fear of Archelaus.

It is also entirely plausible that the family had fled to Egypt out of fear of Archelaus' father, Herod the Great. Egypt was not completely "foreign" to the Jews. There were more Jews living in Alexandria at that time than in Jerusalem or anywhere else in the world. That's where the jobs were. Although Egypt was no longer independent, but a province of Rome, its economy flourished under Rome's umbrella. Joseph, as a carpenter, would have done quite well there, and he need not necessarily have settled in Alexandria, as Jews lived elsewhere as well.

Egypt had long been under the influence of Greek culture, and had been ruled by the Greeks for many years, up until the time of Cleopatra, who was the last Greek Pharaoh. Alexandria was founded by Alexander the Great in 331 BC, hence the name of the city. Ptolemy, Alexander's successor, was an ancestor of Cleopatra, and the patriarch of a long line of Greek Pharaohs, which ended with the suicide of Cleopatra after the defeat of Antony by Octavian's forces about 25 years before the birth of Jesus, at which time Egypt came under Roman rule. At the time of the flight to Egypt, there was good reason to get out of the reach of Herod the Great as quickly as possible. Anyone who had the opportunity to leave who had any sense at all would have done so, whether or not they had become a target of Herod's paranoia. Although he had done much for Israel, Herod became rather demented in his old age. He killed everyone, without hesitation. He killed his favorite wife, he killed her grandfather, he killed her mother, he killed his brother-in-law, and he killed three of his own sons and he killed numerous other subjects whenever he suspected they were a threat to his rule. No one was exempt. He even killed the high priest, who happened to be another one of his brothers-in-law. For Herod to slaughter all of the male babies born within two years at Bethlehem would have been nothing for Herod, as that would amount to around twenty or so, and he had already killed a lot more poor souls than that.

CHAPTER 6

Jewish Culture

1. A BRIEF HISTORY OF THE JEWS

According to Jewish tradition, God created man from the dust of the earth, and gave him the name "Adam," which means "of the soil" (Genesis 2:7). There is a specific spot upon the earth where God gathered up that dust. It is Mount Zion, the place God also chose for His divine presence to rest upon earth ("...Yahweh Sabaoth [God] who dwells on Mount Zion," Isaiah 8:18). And, according to Jewish tradition, it was from this holy place that the entire world took form. That hallowed ground is located in the City of Jerusalem. It is known as "The Temple Mount." The first Temple was built at that precise location by Solomon in the year 957 BC, almost a thousand years before Jesus was born.

The first Temple lasted around four hundred years. It was destroyed by the Babylonians in 586 BC, and the Jews were taken to Babylon in captivity. The Babylonian captivity ended some 60 years later, when they were freed by the King of Persia. The Jews began construction of the Second Temple shortly after their return to Jerusalem.

The Second Temple lasted over five hundred years. Jesus was born during the reign of Herod the Great, toward the end of that period, known as the "Second Temple." The Temple was again destroyed by the Romans in 70 AD as a result of a Jewish revolt, about forty years after the crucifixion of Jesus. The Temple has never been rebuilt. The Temple Mount is now under control of the Moslems, and a mosque has been built in the area where the Temple stood.

Synagogues, which were houses of prayer and communal gathering, existed a long time before destruction of the Second Temple, but while it still stood, communal worship centered around sacrificial offerings in the Temple. The Temple Mount, upon which the Temple was located, remains the holiest site in Judaism. And since the exact location of the Temple itself upon the Temple Mount is uncertain, Jews are forbidden to walk upon those grounds to avoid unintentionally entering the area where the Holy of Holies (the site of the Divine Presence within the Temple) stood. It was from that site that the high priest communicated directly with God, and it was only the high priest who was allowed to enter the area.

During the reign of Herod the Great, the Second Temple flourished. About fifteen years before Jesus was born, Herod the Great further expanded the Temple Mount, the plateau upon which the Temple was built, almost doubling its size. He accomplished this project by constructing huge walls around the site and filling the new sections with earth and rubble. At the southern end of the new section, Herod built the Royal Stoa, in which the city's commercial and legal transactions were conducted. It was

The Historical Perspective

Herod's most magnificent secular construction, and the three-aisled structure was described by Josephus as deserving "to be mentioned better than any other under the sun." That part of the Royal Stoa adjacent to the Temple was most likely the location of Jesus' "Cleansing of the Temple," because it was the site where sacrificial doves could be bought and coins bearing prohibited images could be exchanged.

At the northwestern corner of the expanded plateau (Temple Mount), Herod built the Antonia Fortress, to house the garrison of the Roman Army Auxiliary.

2. WHO WERE THE JEWS?

According to the Bible, Jewish ancestry is traced to the patriarchs Abraham, Isaac and Jacob in the second millennium BC. However, converts to Judaism, with some exceptions, gained status as Jews equal to those born into Judaism, and have been absorbed into the Jewish people throughout the millennia, so that the Jews were at no time a "pure" race. Joseph, one of the twelve sons of Israel, who became the most powerful man in Egypt next to the Pharaoh after he was sold into slavery by his brothers, married the daughter of an Egyptian priest. When famine struck, he brought the sons of Israel down to Egypt, where they were settled in the Land of Goshen. During the next 500 years, the Jews intermarried with Egyptians, until they were led out of Egypt in the Exodus by Moses, who himself had married the daughter of a Midianite.

Herod the Great was only a second generation Jew. His father, Antipater, was a native of Idumea, the land known as Edom in the Old Testament, located southeast of Judea between the Dead Sea and the Gulf of Aqaba. The Old Testament describes the Edomites as descendents of Esau, the eldest son of the Jewish patriarch Isaac. Esau was born with reddish or ruddy skin and red hair (Genesis 25:25) and his descendents also carried those genetic traits. The name Edom means 'red' and the term Edomites means "Red People." Rebekah, Isaac's wife, carried both Esau and Jacob (later known as Israel) in her womb at the same time, and was troubled by the struggle of those two children within her. She consulted Yahweh, and He said to her: "There are two nations in your womb, your issue will be two rival peoples. One nation shall have mastery of the other, and the elder shall serve the younger."

Esau was the first to be born and the "elder."

Another explanation for the name "red people, according to Genesis 25:29-34, is that after the boys grew up, Esau came in from the countryside, exhausted, and asked his brother Jacob for "that red soup there." After a brief negotiation, Easu sold to Jacob his birthright in return for the red lintel soup, "—hence the name given to him, Edom" (Genesis 25:31). Years later, when the brothers had large families and large holdings of livestock, the land could no longer support them both; therefore, Esau left the land of Canaan and settled in the mountain-

The Historical Perspective

ous region of Seir, later known as Edom (Genesis, Chapter 36), and eventually known as Idumea. Years later King David defeated the Edomites in the Valley of Salt and imposed governors on Edom (II Samuel 8:15-18).

The Edomites helped plunder Jerusalem and slaughter the Jews when the Babylonians sent the Jews into exile and destroyed the First Temple. For this reason the Prophets denounced Edom violently (Psalms 137.7; Isaiah 34:5-8). And because of this past butchery, under the Torah, the children born of a marriage between an Israelite and an Edomite could not be admitted to the congregation until the third generation (Deuteronomy 23:8-9), and they were excluded from public worship until then. Thus, Herod the Great, whose father, Antipater, was an Edomite, was excluded, as well as Herod's son, Herod Antipas, who was only of the second generation. Whether or not such discrimination was practiced against those rulers is not known. But it does illustrate the extent of the separation between the Jews and Rome's puppet kings, former citizens of Edom.

Antipater, the father of Herod the Great, ever the opportunist, had converted to Judaism and became a high-ranking official under the Jewish kings during the time of independence before the Roman occupation. When the Roman general Pompey conquered Judea and subjected the Jews to Roman rule, Antipater saw another opportunity, and supported Pompey with food and other resources when he attacked Jerusalem. Antipater was no more loyal to the Roman general Pompey than he had been to the Jewish king, and Antipater aided Julius Caesar in Alexandria when Caesar attacked and defeated Pompey. Antipater's reward was to be made the chief minister of Judea, with the right to collect taxes. And, although reluctantly recognized as a Jew, Antipater's son, Herod the Great, who as king of the Jews had restored the Temple and enlarged the Temple Mount, was never allowed to enter the inner sanctum of the Temple, the Holy of Holies, because he was not descended from the rank of priests.

At the time Jesus came through the gates of Jerusalem on his final journey, Herod Antipas, not to be confused with his grandfather Antipater, was the ruler of Galilee, the native land of Jesus. And it was only by force of the Roman Army that he remained in power, ever since his father, Herod the Great, had been placed upon the throne by vote of the Roman Senate and the legions under the control of General Mark Antony, as stated above. As might be expected, neither Herod the Great, nor his son, Antipas, were considered to be "one of us," by the Jews. They were both foreigners and puppets of Rome, an occupying power. As a matter of interest, it should be noted that Jesus, as a descendent of King David, had a more legitimate claim to the throne than did Antipas. Therefore, it is no surprise that Herod Antipas arrested and imprisoned John the Baptist, a Jew with a large following who posed a possible threat to his government, and later had him executed. Next on the list was Jesus of Nazareth, another Jew popular with the people and with a following that seemed to be increasing day by day. And it was rumored that he was performing miracles and might be claiming to be king of the Jews.

In John 11:43-54 we learn that there was a meeting of the "chief priests and Pharisees" where the general discussion was as follows: "'Here is this man working all these signs,' they said, 'and what action are we taking? If we let him go on in this way everybody will believe in him, and the Romans will come and destroy the Holy Place and our nation.'" One of them, Caiaphas, previously appointed high priest by the Romans, said, 'You don't seem to have grasped the situation at all; you fail to see that it is better for one man to die for the people, than for the whole nation to be destroyed.'" Thus it was that both Rome and the puppet rulers of Judea were anxious to quickly snuff out any sign of popular rebellion.

3. THE SAMARITANS

The Samaritans are another matter. They considered themselves to be more Jewish than the Jews of Judea and Jerusalem, while the Jerusalem Jews considered the Samaritans to be half-breeds at best. There is some justification for that claim, as many "foreigners" had settled in the area of Samaria and intermarried with the local population. Under the Samaritan Torah, the Samaritans claimed their worship was the true religion preserved by those Israelites who remained in the Land of Israel, as opposed to Judaism, which they maintained was a related but altered and amended religion brought back by those returning from exile in Babylon. Prior to the Babylonian Exile, the nation of Israel had been divided into two parts. The northern half retained the name "Israel," while the southern half became known as Judah. It was the Jews from Judah who were taken into captivity by the Babylonians. The Jews in the north remained, and those lands became known as Samaria.

"The Jews who returned to their homeland after the Babylonian Exile would not accept the help of the dwellers of the land, who were later identified as the Samaritans, in the building of the Second Temple of Jerusalem. Consequently, the Samaritans built their own temple in Nāblus (Shechem), at the base of Mount Gerizim, some 25 miles north of Jerusalem. The low esteem that Jews had for the Samaritans was the background of Christ's famous parable of the Good Samaritan (Luke 10:25–37).

The Samaritans derived their name from the Hebrew term which meant "Keepers of the Law." They were a large community, consisting of almost a million citizens up to the time of the late Roman Empire. However, their numbers shrunk dramatically as a result of various revolts against the Romans and conversions to Islam, until today there are less than 1,000 practicing Samaritans.

According to Samaritan tradition, Mount Gerizim, near Nablus on the West Bank, was the original

The Historical Perspective

Holy Place of the Israelites from the time that Joshua conquered the land of Canaan and the tribes of Israel settled the land. The Samaritans claimed that Abraham was commanded by God to offer Isaac, his son, as a sacrifice (Genesis 22:2) on Mount Gerizim, and that this mountain was also the place which God had chosen to establish his name and presence on earth (Deut 12:5). Judaism, however, claims that the correct location is the mountain which became the Temple Mount in Jerusalem. In the Gospel of John, the Samaritan woman tells Jesus that Mount Gerizim is the center of Samaritan worship (John 4:20).

Even Jesus found that the Samaritans could be inhospitable: "As the time approached for him to be taken up to heaven, Jesus resolutely set out for Jerusalem. And he sent messengers on ahead, who went into a Samaritan village to get things ready for him; but the people there did not welcome him, because he was heading for Jerusalem. When the disciples James and John saw this, they asked, "Lord, do you want us to call fire down from heaven to destroy them?" But Jesus turned and rebuked them. Then he and his disciples went to another village" (Luke 9:51-53 NIV). Apparently, the Samaritans did not wish to facilitate a pilgrimage to Jerusalem.

Many of the Palestinians of the West Bank are descendants of those Samaritans who converted to Islam, and, thus, are descendants of the original 12 tribes of Israel, and brothers of their neighboring Jews.

4. THE SANHEDRIN

The Talmud identifies two classes of rabbinical courts called Sanhedrin, a Great Sanhedrin and a Lesser Sanhedrin. Each city could have its own lesser Sanhedrin of 23 judges, but there could be only one Great Sanhedrin of 71. The Great Sanhedrin, generally referred to as the Sanhedrin, was located in Jerusalem, and was the Supreme Court and legislative body of the land. At the time of the trial of Jesus, the Sanhedrin met in the Hall of Hewn Stones, built into the north wall of the Temple Mount, half inside the sanctuary and half outside, with doors providing access both to the Temple and to the city. In the case of Jesus' trial, it may have been only necessary for a 23-member panel (functioning as a Lesser Sanhedrin) to convene. In general, the full panel of 71 judges was only convened on matters of national significance (e.g., a declaration of war) or in the event that the 23-member panel could not reach a verdict.

The high priests were the chief religious officials of the Israelite nation. Originally, they belonged to the priestly families descended from Aaron, the first high priest and elder brother of Moses. This practice changed somewhat under Herod the Great, who appointed the high priests from other families. At the time of Jesus of Nazareth, it is almost certain that the high priest was also the chief presiding officer of the Sanhedrin, as this was during Roman times (Josephus, *Jewish Antiquities,* 20:10).

The Historical Perspective

When Pompey captured Jerusalem earlier, he had restored Hyrcanus to the office of high priest and also made him governor of the Jewish nation. Later, when Herod the Great was made king by the Romans, he was given authority to appoint high priests. When Archelaus, Herod's son, was installed by the Romans as ruler of the nation, he also continued to appoint the high priest, and when Archelaus was deposed by the Romans in AD 6, they took over government of the Jews, and it was the Roman Prefect who then appointed the high priests. According to Josephus, under the Roman Prefect, the high priest was entrusted with the dominion of the nation.

Joseph Caiaphas, the Roman-appointed high priest who is said to have organized the plot to kill Jesus, also presided over the Sanhedrin at the trial of Jesus. Thus it was that the Romans had complete control over the Jewish nation, including the Sanhedrin and the priesthood at the time of Jesus' trial.

As another example of Rome's power over the Jews, Annas was appointed by Quirinius, the Roman governor of Syria, as the first high priest of the newly formed Roman province of Judea in 6 AD after the Romans deposed Archelaus, one of the sons of Herod the Great. Annas served as high priest until 14 AD, when at the age of 36 he was deposed by the prefect Gratus for imposing and executing capital sentences which had been forbidden by Rome. But Annas remained as one of the Jews most influential leaders through the use of his five sons and his son-

in-law, Joseph Caiaphas, as Roman-appointed puppet high priests.

Ananias son of Nedebaios (Josephus, *Antiquities*
20:5.2), called "Ananias" in the Book of Acts, Chapter
23, was the high priest who presided during the trial
of Paul at Jerusalem and Caesarea. He officiated as
high priest from about AD 47 to 59. Quadratus, Roman governor of Syria, accused him of being responsible for acts of violence, and he was sent to Rome for
trial (AD 52), but was acquitted by the emperor
Claudius, demonstrating again just how much the
religious and political leaders of the Jews were indebted to Rome for their jobs. As a representative of
Roman rule, Ananias was among the first of those
assassinated by the Jewish people in 66 AD at the
beginning of the great Jewish revolt that resulted in
the destruction of the city and Temple.

5. THE JEWISH RELIGION

At the time of Jesus there were three major Jewish religious groups throughout the land: the Sadducees, the Pharisees, and the Essenes. Although a minority group, the Sadducees were in power and controlled the Sanhedrin. The most interesting aspect of
the religion of the Sadducees is that it is difficult to
admit that it is a religion at all. They did not believe
in a soul which survived death of the body, nor in an
afterlife, nor in a possible resurrection of the body or
soul. Apparently, this sect first appeared during the
2nd century BC, less than two hundred years before

The Historical Perspective

Jesus was born. The sect consisted of Jews from the upper social and economic classes. The Sadducees controlled Jewish politics and religion, including maintaining the Temple, until the destruction of Jerusalem in 70 AD, at which time, they became extinct.

The Sadducees believed that souls died with the body, and in a strict interpretation of the Torah, and placed little or no faith in the books of the prophets or other books of the Old Testament. And, although they held strict control of the country, so far as was permitted by the Romans, they moderated their views at the public level, in order not to antagonize the population, which largely believed in an afterlife and a soul separate from the body. Sadducees, the controlling members of the Sanhedrin and the priesthood, were apparently the ones actively seeking the crucifixion of Jesus, whose views were popular with the people, and who represented a threat to both their puppet government and the dominion of Rome.

Jesus was clearly not a member of this sect or class, and it is interesting to note that Luke 20:27-40 relates an incident where some Sadducees, "those who say that there is no resurrection," attempted to trap Jesus through the example of possible conflict in the afterlife where a man had taken a second wife after death of the first.

The Pharisees were the largest sect throughout the land during the 1st century AD, although they were not in control of the government or the Temple. However, after the destruction of Jerusalem and the

JESUS OF NAZARETH

Temple in 70 AD, the Pharisee conception of religion became the established Rabbinic Judaism, and the Sadducees disappeared from the scene.

The early Christians shared several beliefs of the Pharisees, such as resurrection, retribution in the next world, angels, human freedom and Divine Providence. Some scholars have speculated that Jesus himself was a Pharisee, which is questionable, considering his many attacks against them throughout the gospels. Nor is there any evidence that the Pharisee sect existed in Galilee. Paul, however, certainly had been a Pharisee, as he stated.

The third group were the Essenes, apocalyptic (belief that the world will come to an end very soon) ascetics with a significant following, although never mentioned in the New Testament. Several scholars believe that Jesus was an Essene, or at least had some close attachment to them. The glossary, prepared by the editors, of the book by Pope Benedict XVI on Jesus states that "it appears that not only John the Baptist, but possibly Jesus and his family as well, were close to the Qumran [home of the Essenes] community, though the teaching of John and of Jesus differed significantly from that of the Qumran community" (Joseph Ratzinger, *Jesus of Nazareth Part Two, Holy Week: From the Entrance Into Jerusalem To The Resurrection,* Ignatius Press).

Again, this is not the statement of Pope Benedict XVI, but his editors at Ignatius Press. No sources are cited for this conclusion, and one wonders whether it is likely that the Holy Family had any connection

The Historical Perspective

with this sect which appears to be responsible for the Dead Sea Scrolls, and which lived a considerable distance away, across Samaria and Judea. However, some members of this sect lived elsewhere throughout Palestine, so it is possible.

The Jewish historian, Josephus, devotes a large section of his two books on the Jews to the Essenes, a group which appear to have much in common with early Christian views and practices. They taught the immortality of the soul, and that the rewards of righteousness were to be earnestly sought. They held all things in common, so that a rich man enjoyed no more of his own wealth than a man who had nothing at all. They carried nothing with them when they traveled, as other members of the sect throughout the land shared what they had with them. And in every city where they lived, someone was appointed to take care of strangers and provide garments and other necessities for them. Their creed was to assist those who want, and to show mercy. They were restrained and faithful, and ministers of peace, and spent a great deal of time studying the writings of the ancients.

No one was immediately admitted to the sect. First, he must live according to a prescribed method for one year, during which time he was given a white garment to wear and his conduct was supervised. Once he had given evidence that he could observe their way of living, he was put to the test for another two years, partook of the waters of purification, and was then admitted into their society (Josephus, *Jew-*

ish War, 2:18 and *Antiquities,* 18:1).

A fourth group, with a more aggressive spirit, originated during the final years of Herod the Great, and were known as the Zealots. They passionately resented the subjugation of "God's people" to the foreign power of Rome. In the year 6 AD they started a revolt under the reckless leadership of Judas of Galilee, when the Romans undertook a census of the Jews. The result was an invasion of Galilee by Roman Legions from Syria, just over the border, and the total destruction of Sepphoris, the administrative, religious and commercial center of Galilee. Sepphoris was an hour's walk from Nazareth, the home of Jesus, who at that time was about 11 years old. Jesus was old enough to observe the smoke rising from the ashes of that city on the plain below, less than four miles northwest of Nazareth. And Jesus could well have assisted his father Joseph, the carpenter, in the rebuilding of the capital city to its former glory in the years following its destruction. There could also have been a major concern within the family of Jesus at Nazareth as the city burned, because according to Christian tradition, his grandparents, Anna and Joachim, the parents of his mother, Mary, were natives of Sepphoris.

With good reason, hot heads from Galilee were always under suspicion since they were responsible for the Roman destruction of Sepphoris. Then again there was more immediate trouble with men from Galilee, as reported in Luke 13:1-4. Just prior to his triumphant entry into Jerusalem some people came

The Historical Perspective

"and told Jesus about the Galileans whose blood Pilate had mixed with their sacrifices." And it was the Zealots from Galilee who once again started the final Jewish revolt less than forty years after the crucifixion, resulting in the total destruction of the Second Temple and the City of Jerusalem itself.

6. THE JEWISH LANGUAGE

"It is generally agreed that Aramaic was the common language of Israel in the first century AD" (Allen C. Myers, ed. *The Eerdmans Bible Dictionary*. p. 72). It is also the language in which the Gospel of Matthew was originally written.

Long before the time of Jesus, Aramaic was the common language throughout the Middle East. But by the 3rd century BC, Greek had overtaken Aramaic, and become the international language of administration and trade. The Greek language also displaced Aramaic as the common language in Egypt and Syria, while Aramaic, the language spoken by Jesus, continued as the language of the common people throughout the greater area of Judaea. Hebrew, the language of the ancient Jews, was limited to religious services.

Although Latin was the language of the Roman army, it had no impact on the local language, and Greek was the language used by the Romans when communicating with the local leaders. Thus, Greek was a second language of many Jews. Since it was the international language of literature and commerce, the New Testament, with the exception of the first versions of Matthew, was written in Greek.

Often portrayed as an illiterate peasant (treated later), Jesus was obviously a well-educated man who spoke Aramaic as his native language, as well as Greek, and read and spoke Hebrew. When he was only 12 years old, he sat in the Temple at Jerusalem and discussed scripture with the doctors (Luke 2:41-50). The scriptures were in Hebrew, and perhaps the discussions as well. At Nazareth, he read scripture (as he apparently usually did), and was handed the scroll of the prophet Isaiah (Hebrew Bible), from which he read to the assembly (Luke 4:16-30). Jesus also taught at the synagogue in Capernaum (Luke 2:31-37), and synagogues elsewhere where his status as a teacher was not questioned. Finally, although his discussions with members of the Sanhedrin at his hearing were probably in Aramaic, his conversations with Pontius Pilate were most likely in Greek, the international language of that day, much as English is the international language of today. There was no need for Pontius Pilate to learn the local language, and he probably never did. He had been in the area only a few years as prefect, and his Jewish counterparts spoke the international Greek language. In addition, Pontius Pilate did not live among the Jews, but in the Roman Province of Caesarea on the coast, located mid-way between present Tel Aviv and Haifa. At that time, the population of Caesarea consisted almost entirely of gentiles of Greek and Roman origin.

The Historical Perspective

Hebrew, as used in Jerusalem today, had not been spoken in Israel for several centuries. It was the language of the Old Testament, and considered blasphemous to be used outside of religious services. However, Hebrew was revived as the spoken language of modern Israel beginning in the 19th century, primarily because of the many dialects and languages spoken by returning Jews. As a result, Aramaic is no longer spoken, and Hebrew and Arabic are the two official languages of the nation.

CHAPTER 7

Josephus

Since much of what we know outside the Bible about Jewish society during the life of Jesus comes from Josephus, it is appropriate to make a few notes regarding that well-respected historian.

Josephus was what has commonly been referred to as a Hellenistic Jew, that is, someone who believed that Judaism and Graeco-Roman thought and culture were compatible. His most important works were *The Jewish War*, written around 75 AD, an account of the Jewish revolt that resulted in the destruction of the Temple and the City of Jerusalem in 70 AD, and *Antiquities of the Jews*, written in 94 AD. The *Antiquities* gives a detailed history of the world from the Jewish perspective, and was written for a Roman audience. Both of these works, with many overlapping accounts, are a valuable source of insight into first century Judaism as well as the world background at the time of Jesus.

The father of Josephus was a priest from Jerusalem. His mother was an aristocratic woman descended from the ruling Jewish kings who were in power at the time Judea was conquered by the Roman General Pompey. It was an extremely wealthy and powerful family.

Born and raised in Jerusalem, Josephus was educated there. When he was in his early twenties, he was sent to Rome to negotiate with the Emperor,

The Historical Perspective

Nero, for the release of several Jewish priests, who apparently were suspected revolutionaries. After a successful completion of this mission, he returned home to find that the Jews at home were actually starting a revolt against the Romans. At this young age, Josephus was put in charge of the Jewish forces in Galilee. The Jewish campaign in Galilee ended in defeat, and the Romans killed thousands. Josephus, however, fled to a cave with about forty of his soldiers.

The Roman legions in pursuit were commanded by Flavius Vespasian and his son Titus (both of whom subsequently became Roman emperors). Once the Romans learned where he was holed up, they asked Josephus to surrender. At that time, he was apparently one of the few survivors in the cave. Josephus surrendered and became a prisoner. He must have been known to the Romans through the earlier role he played in negotiating with Nero, as Josephus, ever the survivor, went over to the other side, and became one of the negotiators on behalf of the Romans with the defending Jews during the siege of Jerusalem in the year 70. However, called a traitor, he had no credibility with the Jews behind the walls, was unable to persuade the defenders of Jerusalem to surrender to the Roman siege, and instead became a witness to the destruction of the city and the Holy Temple.

The following year, 71 AD, Josephus arrived in Rome with Titus, where he became a Roman citizen under the patronage of the Flavian family. He was given the Roman first name of Titus and family name of Flavius, which was standard practice. Josephus' wife had been killed during the siege of Jerusalem, along with his parents, and Vespasian arranged for Josephus to marry a captured Jewish woman, who promptly left him. He next married an Alexandrian Jewish woman as his third wife, whom he divorced after three sons were born, and during the year 75 AD, he married a Greek Jewish woman from Crete as his fourth wife, and finally found happiness. They had two sons.

It was while living the good life at court with the Flavian emperors that Josephus wrote his first work, the history of the war he had been involved in. He first wrote in his native language of Aramaic, then translated it into Greek (the language of the eastern part of the Empire) to flatter his patrons and for the purpose that they could use it to warn against the folly of opposing Roman rule. The book was published in Greek when he was about forty years old. A few years later, he undertook a massive work in Greek (*Antiquities*) for the purpose of explaining to his Roman audience the history of the Jews. This second major work was published when he was about 56 years old. He wrote other books, including the autobiography of his life from the time of his birth to his writing of the *Antiquities*. It is assumed he died in the year 100 AD, although the exact year of his death is unknown.

CHAPTER 8

Reflections upon the Gospels
Based upon a study by
Benjamin Rush Rhees

The following exposition is based substantially on *The Life of Jesus of Nazareth, a Study* by Benjamin Rush Rhees, Charles Scribner's Sons, 1900. Rhees was the president of the University of Rochester from 1900-1935. He earned his undergraduate degree from Amherst College, and was ordained a Baptist minister after he graduated from the Hartford Theological Seminary.

Although his writing is cumbersome, redundant, and often difficult to follow, Rhees' work is recommended for further reading as a neglected masterpiece, far surpassing many of the more modern studies of the life of Jesus of Nazareth. It is a vivid commentary on the life of Jesus and the important events of his ministry.

Other modern sources, too numerous to mention, have been used to edit and expand upon the original study by Rhees to the extent that the following may be considered to be an original and up-to-date analysis of the gospels.

JESUS OF NAZARETH

1. THE SYNOPTIC GOSPELS.

The Synoptic Gospels are Matthew, Mark and Luke. These first three gospels are so alike that they can be viewed as if they were one. For that reason they are called "synoptic" which means "with one eye." According to Christian tradition, Matthew the publican (tax collector), one of the Apostles, was the first to write an account of the life of Jesus, and he wrote his gospel at Palestine in Aramaic for Christians who converted from Judaism. His gospel was translated into Greek later.

Mark was a disciple from Jerusalem who assisted Paul in his apostolic work, and later Peter. Mark served Peter both as clerk and interpreter, and wrote down Peter's teachings in the gospel known as Mark.

Luke, another disciple, was probably not a Jew. He was born at Antioch. He was a physician, and he was with Paul on his second and third missions, as well as his two Roman captivities. Therefore, his gospel can claim the authority of Paul, just as Mark's gospel can claim the authority of Peter. Luke also wrote the Acts of the Apostles.

The first gospel (Matthew) leaves the reader with a clear sense of the development of Jesus' ministry. Matthew begins his narrative with an account of the birth of Jesus, the ministry of John the Baptist, and Jesus' baptism, temptation, and withdrawal into Galilee. He then tells us about the teachings of Jesus concerning the law of the kingdom of heaven, then a series of great miracles confirming the new doctrine,

The Historical Perspective

then the expansion of the ministry and deepening hostility of the Pharisees, leading to the parables, and the final withdrawal from Galilee to the north. Jesus' ministry is met with popular enthusiasm in the beginning, then comes a chilling and decline of support, but with the winning of a few solid hearts to his mission.

Matthew next leads us to Jerusalem, where Jesus is victorious in seeming defeat (16:21 to 28:20). Matthew wishes to convince men that Jesus is Israel's Messiah, therefore he emphasizes the fulfillment of prophecy. The emphasis which this gospel gives to the death of Jesus and to his resurrection, as God's seal of approval of him, forms a forcible argument to prove the Messiahship of Jesus, not simply in spite of his rejection by the Jews, but by using that very rejection as the vehicle leading to God's vindication of the crucified one. Matthew, while proving that Jesus is the Messiah promised to Israel, recognizes clearly the freedom of the new faith from the bonds of Judaism. The choice of Galilee for the Messianic ministry (4:12-17), the comment of Jesus on the faith of the centurion (8:10-12), the rebuke of Israel in the parable of the Wicked Husbandmen (21:33-46), and especially the last commission of the risen Lord ("Go, therefore, make disciples of all the nations," 28:18-20), show that this gospel sought to convince the Jews not only that Jesus is Messiah, but also that as Messiah he came to bring salvation to all the world.

The second gospel, Mark, is much simpler in construction, while presenting essentially the same picture of the ministry as is found in Matthew. To its simplicity, Mark adds a vividness of narration to his account, which probably represents most accurately the actual course of the life of Jesus. While it reports fewer incidents and teachings than either of the others, a comparison with Matthew and Luke shows a preference in Mark for Jesus' deeds, though addresses are not lacking. The whole narrative is animated in style and full of graphic details. The story of Jesus seems to be reproduced from a memory of fresh personal impressions of events as they occurred. Examples are the frequent comments on the effect of Jesus' ministry, such as "We have never seen anything like this" (2:12), or "He has done all things well" (7:37), and the introduction into the narrative of Aramaic words, such as "Talitha, kum!" which means, "Little girl, I tell you to get up."

There is no artificial plan to Mark. It is a straight -forward collection of annals fresh from the living memory, which present the actual Jesus teaching and healing, and going on his way to the cross and resurrection. After the briefest possible reference to the ministry of John the Baptist and the baptism and temptation of Jesus (1:1-13), this gospel proceeds to set forth the ministry in Galilee (1:14 to 9:50). The narrative then follows Jesus to Jerusalem, and closes with his crucifixion and resurrection.

The third gospel, Luke, is more nearly a biography than Matthew or Mark. It opens with a preface stating that after a study of many earlier attempts to record the life of Jesus the author has undertaken to present as complete an account as possible of that life from the beginning. The book is addressed to one Theophilus, apparently a Greek Christian, and its chief aim is practical—to confirm his conviction concerning matters of faith. Luke states that after carefully going over the whole story from the beginning, he has decided to write an orderly account for Theophilus, so that he might learn how well founded the teaching is that he has already received. From this we may presume that Luke had prior discussions with Theophilus, or exchanged prior letters with him, and wished to expand upon what Theophilus had learned concerning Jesus and his mission. Luke's interest in the completeness of his account is apparent from the beginning, where he reports incidents which occur prior to the birth of John the Baptist and Jesus, such as the annunciation to Mary and her visitation with Elizabeth, the mother of John the Baptist.

Due to Luke's desire for such completeness we are indebted to him for much of the story of Jesus, which is otherwise unrecorded. Like the first two gospels, Luke represents the ministry of Jesus as beginning in Galilee, and carried on there until the final tragedy at Jerusalem. It is in connection with the journey to Jerusalem that Luke inserts most of the incidents which are found only in his gospel. His account of the rejection at Jerusalem, the crucifixion, and resurrection follow mainly the same lines as Matthew and Mark, although he may have gained his knowledge of many particulars from different sources.

It is characteristic of Luke to name Jesus "Lord" more often than either of his predecessors. And in Luke there is a noticeable emphasis on Jesus' ministry of compassion; here more than in any other gospel he is pictured as the friend of sinners. Moreover, we owe chiefly to Luke our knowledge of Jesus as a man of prayer and as subject to repeated temptation. This revelation increases our confidence in the accuracy of Luke's description of Jesus. His gospel is very full of comfort to those living in poverty, though it does not exalt poverty for its own sake. While our first gospel, Matthew, pictures Jesus as the fulfillment of God's promises to his people, and Mark portrays Jesus as the man of power at work before our very eyes, Luke sets before us the Lord ministering with divine compassion to men subject to like temptations as himself, though, unlike them, he knew no sin.

The first three gospels agree concerning the locality and progress of his Messianic work, and the form and contents of his teaching, showing, in fact, verbal identity in many parts of their narrative. Although they differ in the order in which they arrange some of the events in Jesus' life, they often agree to the letter in their report of deeds or words of Jesus. Yet from beginning to end, remarkable differences stand side by side with remarkable identities. Some of the identities of language suggest that they have used, at least in part, the same previously existing written record. In many places, the sentence structure is ex-

The Historical Perspective

actly the same, where, under normal circumstances, no two authors would have written the sentence in the same way. One of the clearest examples of this is found in the insertion, at the same place in each of the three accounts of the comment "then he said to the paralytic" which interrupts the words of Jesus in the cure of the paralytic (Mark 2:10; Matt. 9:6; Luke 5:24).

When the three gospels are carefully compared, it appears that Mark contains very little that is not found in Matthew and Luke. However, when comparing Matthew's arrangement of the first half of his account with the gospel of Mark, it becomes apparent that the order in the first part of Matthew has been determined by other than the chronological considerations of Mark. Nevertheless, it is fair to say that the gospel of Mark reveals the framework on which all three of the Synoptic Gospels are constructed, although Mark's chronology is most likely a condensed version of events which took place over several years. Another interesting fact is that the matters which Matthew and Luke have in common, which are not found in Mark, consists almost entirely of teachings and addresses. And each gospel has some other matters peculiar to itself.

It is also interesting to note that not one of these gospels contains any statement concerning the identity of its author. We are indebted to later tradition for the names by which we know them. The earliest reference to our gospels, outside of the gospels themselves, comes from Papias, a bishop of the Church at

Hierapolis (Pamukkale, Southwestern Turkey) in the second century. His book *Interpretations of the Sayings of the Lord (logia)* is also good authority for the existence of the oral "Sayings of Jesus," some of which are recorded in Matthew and Luke.

Unfortunately his book has not survived. Its existence is known only through fragments quoted by later writers. Papias was also one of the early authorities for the claim that Matthew was first written in Aramaic. There is some speculation that Papias had met John, and that Papias was writing as an old man around the year 110, and that his information came from his earlier years, for which reason some of his sources could have known Jesus or the Apostles, or both (Hill, Charles E. *"Papias of Hierapolis,"* The Expository Times, 2006, p.309).

Papias reports that an earlier teacher had said, "Mark, having become the interpreter of Peter, wrote down accurately, though not, indeed, in order, whatsoever he remembered of the things said or done by Christ, for he neither heard the Lord nor followed him, but afterward, as I said, he followed Peter, who adapted his teachings to the needs of his hearers, but with no intention of giving a connected account of the Lord's discourses. So that Mark committed no error when he thus wrote some things as he remembered them, for he was careful of one thing, not to omit any of the things which he had heard and not to state any of them falsely." (Eusebius, *Church History*. iii. 39, translation and commentary by Paul L. Maier, p. 114).

The Historical Perspective

The result of many years' study by scholars of all shades of opinion is the very general conclusion that the writing which Papias attributed to Mark was essentially what we now have in the New Testament.

It is also almost universally acknowledged that the work ascribed by Papias to the Apostle Matthew cannot be our first gospel because its language does not have the characteristics which other translations from Aramaic lead us to expect. The relation of our gospels to the two books mentioned by Papias may be best summarized as follows: The earliest gospel writing of which we know anything was a collection of the teachings of Jesus made by the apostle Matthew, in which he collected and wrote down with simple narrative introductions, those sayings of the Lord which from the beginning had passed from mouth to mouth in the circle of the disciples. At a later time Mark wrote down the account of the ministry of Jesus which Peter had been accustomed to relate in his apostolic preaching. The work of the apostle Matthew, while much richer in the sayings of Jesus, lacked the completeness that characterizes a narrative; therefore it occurred to some early disciple of Matthew or Mark to blend together these two primitive gospel records, adding such other items of knowledge as came to his hand from oral tradition or written memoranda. As his aim was practical rather than historical, he added such editorial comments as would make the new gospel an argument for the Messiahship of Jesus. Since the most precious element in this new gospel, which we now know as Matthew, was the apostolic record of the teachings of the Lord, the name of Matthew and not of his literary successor and editor, was given to the book.

The third gospel is ascribed by tradition to Luke, the companion of Paul. The author himself says that he made use of such earlier records as were accessible, among which the chief seems to have been the writings of Mark and the apostle Matthew. To Luke's industry, however, we owe our knowledge of many incidents and teachings from the life of Jesus which are not contained in those two other records. Some of those Luke doubtless found in written form, and some he gathered from oral testimony. His close agreement with Mark suggests that he used Mark as his chronological framework and the rich materials which he had gathered from Matthew and other sources to make a new gospel, the most complete of any written up to his time.

The dates of these first three gospels can be only approximately known. It is probable that the "logia" collected by the apostle Matthew, and upon which the Synoptic gospels are largely based, as related by Papias, were written not long after the crucifixion, and it is certain that the Gospel of Mark dates from before the fall of Jerusalem in the year 70 AD. Our first complete gospel, the re-written Matthew, must have been made between 50 and 70 AD, and the Gospel of Luke may be dated about the year 80—all within thirty to fifty years after the crucifixion of Jesus.

The Historical Perspective

2. THE GOSPEL OF JOHN

John, the fourth gospel claims an unnamed eye-witness, one of the disciples, to authenticate the events it relates. But nowhere is this person connected directly to John, one of the first two disciples of Jesus. Whoever it may be, this eyewitness, not necessarily the author, took part in the Passion, saw the empty tomb, and saw the risen Christ. This fourth gospel is much more complete than the first three, and is far more concerned with the significance of the events in the life of Jesus and all that he did and said. It also places great stress on the need for unity and mutual love.

The gospel is closely related in style to the three surviving Epistles of John such that commentators treat the four books together (See the *Jerusalem Bible, Introduction to the Gospel and Letters of Saint John).* However, according to many scholars, John was not the author of any of these books. "Although ancient traditions attributed to the Apostle John the fourth gospel, the Book of Revelation, and the three Epistles of John, modern scholars believe that he wrote none of them" (Harris, Stephen. *Understanding the Bible* p. 355). If John were written close to the end of the first century, John must have been around 100 years old at the time. This is explained by some scholars with the remark that he was asked to write the book by church elders, or did so on his own volition, but never finished it. This seems to make sense, and scholars are no longer looking for the identity of a single writer but for numerous others whose writings and revisions have been absorbed into the gospel's development over a period of time and in several stages (Geza Vermes, *The authentic gospel of Jesus,* London, Penguin Books. 2004. A note on sources, p. x-xvii).

Since the author of John is stated to be a witness to the events related, it is assumed that John was, therefore, present inside the Sanhedrin during that hearing. When Jesus was arrested and taken before Annas and Caiaphas, we learn that "Simon Peter, with another disciple, followed Jesus." But was this other disciple John? "This disciple, who was known to the high priest, went with Jesus into the high priest's palace, but Peter stayed outside the door. So the other disciple, the one known to the high priest, went out, spoke to the woman who was keeping the door and brought Peter in" (John 18:15). Notes to this passage in various study Bibles state that this disciple was probably John the Evangelist. But with all due respect to those editors, how would John have gained access to the Sanhedrin in the first place? And how would John be known to the high priest? John was one of the first four disciples, and he and his brother, James, were sons of Zebedee. They were fisherman, and in their boat, mending their nets when Jesus called to them (Matthew 4:18-22). So, is it likely that John, a simple fisherman from Galilee to the north would be known to the high priest, and possibly a member of the Sanhedrin? Possible—yes. His family could have been very influential fishermen and owners of a large fleet. But there is a much more logical and probable solution to the question. This disciple "known to the high priest" could be Joseph of Arimathea. He was a member of the Sanhedrin and would have been present at the hearing. The high priest, who was the presiding officer over the Sanhedrin, would certainly have known him. And we know that Joseph of Arimathea was referred to as a disciple from the following: "Joseph of Arimathea, who was a disciple of Jesus—though a secret one because he was afraid of the Jews—asked Pilate to let him remove the body of Jesus" (John 19:38). Thus, it is reasonable to conclude that John is an authentic gospel, though there is no direct evidence in the gospel or elsewhere that the disciple John wrote the final version of the gospel, and the reasonable conclusion is that he did not. John, as well as John's disciples, would have learned from Peter the details of the trial inside the Sanhedrin, and John likely wrote down what Peter had told him. Finally, this fourth gospel was not published by John himself, but by his disciples after his death. The entry at John, 21:24, makes this clear. When referring to the disciple who had asked Jesus at the Last Supper who would betray him, generally understood to have been John, the final editors of John conclude: "This disciple is the one who vouches for these things and has written them down, and we [his disciples] know that his testimony is true."

What is reported in John, however, gives us a picture of Jesus in contrast to the first three. Matthew,

JESUS OF NAZARETH

Mark and Luke present the works of Jesus and his teachings concerning the kingdom of God and human conduct, leaving the truth concerning the teacher himself to be inferred. John opens the heart of Jesus and makes him disclose his thought about himself. This gospel is avowedly an argument: "There were many other signs that Jesus worked and the disciples saw, but they are not recorded in this book. These are recorded so that you may believe that Jesus is the Christ, the Son of God, and that believing this you may have life through his name" (John 20:30-31). Its selection of material is admitted to be partial. Its aim is to confirm the faith of Christians in the heavenly nature and saving power of their Lord; and its method is that of appeal to testimony, to signs, and to his own self-disclosures.

The opening verses of John are of an abstract theological nature. The body of the gospel, however, consists of a succession of incidents and teachings which follow each other like a collection of annals, with some exceptions. The theme of the gospel is the self-disclosure of Jesus. As the gospel is an argument, John does not hesitate to mingle his own comments with his report of Jesus' words. The Christ whom John portrays is the Master who has entered into his experience as a living influence. The Son of God is for John the human Jesus. The Word who was made flesh, so that men through him might become the sons of God.

The final entry in John is compelling reason to think that the ministry of Jesus may well have lasted several years. John 21:25 states that: "There were many other things that Jesus did; and if all were written down, the world itself, I suppose, would not hold all the books that would have to be written."

Now it is true that in portions of Matthew and Luke there are various allusions most easily understood if it is assumed that Jesus visited Jerusalem before his appearance there at the end of his ministry. Such, for example, are the parable of the Good Samaritan (Luke 10:25-37), the story of the visit to Mary and Martha (Luke 10:38-42), and the lamentation of Jesus over Jerusalem (Luke 13:34-35; Matt, 23:37-39). All three of the Synoptic Gospels also agree in attributing to emissaries from Jerusalem much of the hostility manifested against Jesus in his Galilean ministry (Luke 5:17; Mark 3:22; Matt. 15:1; Mark 7:1), which can only mean some personal experience with Jesus in Jerusalem before his final entrance. The Synoptics also presuppose an acquaintance of Jesus with households in and near Jerusalem not easy to explain if he never visited Judea before his passion. This suggests that the narrative of Mark does not tell the whole story, a conclusion in accordance with the account of his work given by Papias. It has been assumed that Peter, the source for Mark, was a Galilean, a man of family living in Capernaum. It is possible that on some of the earlier visits of Jesus to Jerusalem Peter did not accompany his Master, and in reporting the things which he knew he naturally confined himself to his own experiences.

We have in our gospel records, therefore, two authorities for the general course of the ministry of Jesus, Mark and John. And even if John, the fourth gospel should be proved not to be the work of John himself, its picture of the ministry of Jesus must be recognized as coming from some apostolic source.

The first and third gospels (Matthew and Luke) furnish us from various sources rich additions to Mark's narrative, and it is to Matthew, Luke, and John that we turn chiefly for the teachings of Jesus. As Rhees cautions us, however, each gospel should be read keeping in mind its incompleteness, and remembering also the particular purpose and individual enthusiasm for Jesus which produced it.

3. OTHER RECORDS OF THE LIFE OF JESUS

In addition to the gospels, there are other claimants for recognition as original records from the life of Jesus. One example is that word of the Lord which Paul quoted to the Ephesian elders at Miletus, "There is more happiness in giving than receiving" (Acts 20:35).

Other verses of the traditional English text no longer supported by the best Greek manuscripts have been omitted in the NIV. For example Matthew 17:21 which in the King James version reads: "Howbeit (however) this kind goeth not out but by prayer and fasting," a saying by Jesus referring to those who can move mountains even though their faith is only that of a mustard seed.

The Historical Perspective

Scattered here and there in writings of the apostolic and succeeding ages are other sayings attributed to Jesus which, although long included in the gospels, now have a questionable standing in the New Testament. The most important of them is the story of the woman taken in adultery (John 7:53 to 8:11), which may well give a true incident from Jesus' life, but is now set off in brackets or in italics in some printings of the NIV to indicate their uncertain status. They may represent the "many other" things which John and the original gospels have referenced, but their small number proves that our gospels have preserved for us practically all that was known of Jesus from the first witnesses to his life.

The other class of claimants is of a quite different character—the so-called Apocryphal Gospels. These consist chiefly of legends connected with the birth and early years of Jesus, and with his death and resurrection. They are for the most part crude tales that have entirely mistaken the real character of the one whom they claim to exalt, and need only to be read to be rejected.

[Note: The word "apocrypha" means "things put away" or "things hidden" and comes from the Greek. The term is usually applied to the books that were considered by the Church as not divinely inspired, and thus not canonical, although they may have had some value. In general terms today, the accepted meaning is that such books are probably false, and at the least, are unreliable (the so-called Secret Gospel of Mark, discussed later, is a good example). On the other hand, the Council of Trent declared that the Latin Vulgate, which includes the adultery episode in John 7:53-8:11, was authentic and authoritative. The passage describes a confrontation between Jesus and the scribes and Pharisees over whether a woman, caught in an act of adultery, ought to be stoned. Jesus shames the crowd into dispersing, and averts the execution ("Let he who is without sin throw the first stone"). It is only recent reviews of ancient Greek manuscripts which have now brought into question the standing of these passages in the textual history of the New Testament.]

Another interesting thought is that writers of fiction also existed in the days of antiquity. What they wrote is commonly referred to as prose, which presumably places it on a higher level than our current pulp fiction. But if someone had written a narrative purely for purposes of entertainment, and only fragments of parchment remained of the fictional story, we can assume that, as long as it were proven to be around 2,000 years old, someone would be parading it before the world as another recently discovered revelation. In the days of antiquity, it was also a common practice for an unknown author to make literary use of another's name—a well known personage—to obtain acceptance, especially of inferior work. Therefore, one must be careful when blindly accepting newly discovered manuscripts on the basis of age alone.

CHAPTER 9

The Ministry of Jesus
by
Benjamin Rush Rhees
Edited and supplemented by Charles Daudert

Any theory that the ministry of Jesus lasted little more than one year is plagued with difficulties that seem insurmountable. The first problem is presented by the three Passovers distinctly mentioned in the Gospel of John (2:13, cleansing of the Temple, 6:4, the miracle of the loaves shortly before the Jewish feast of Passover, and 12:1, six days before the Passover, Jesus went to Bethany). The last of these is plainly identical with the only one named in the other gospels. The second Passover in John gives the time of year for the feeding of the five thousand, and agrees with the mention of "the green grass" in the account of Mark and Matthew. John's first Passover falls in a section which demands a place before Mark 1:14, "After John [the Baptist] had been arrested, Jesus went into Galilee (compare John 3:22-24, "After [baptism] Jesus went with his disciples into the Judean countryside and stayed with them there and baptized.... This was before John had been put in prison"). It must be shown that this first Passover is chronologically out of order in John, or the "one-year ministry" is impossible. The fact that at this Passover Jesus cleansed the Temple, and that the other gospels assign such a cleansing to the close of the ministry, suggests the possibility that John has set it at the opening of his narrative for reasons connected with his argument. This interpretation falls, however, before the perfect simplicity of structure of John's narrative. The transitions from incident to incident in this gospel are those of simple succession, and indicate, on the writer's part, no suspicion that he was contradicting notions concerning the ministry of Jesus familiar to his contemporaries.

Whatever the conclusion reached concerning the authorship of the gospel of John, the fact that it gained acceptance very early as apostolic would seem to prove that its conception of the length of Jesus' ministry was not opposed to the recognized apostolic testimony. It is safe to conclude, therefore, that time must be allowed in Jesus' ministry for at least three Passover celebrations.

Most modern studies of this question conclude with at least three Passover seasons. For some, however, a ministry as long as three years also presents difficulties, for all that is told in the four gospels could cover but a small fraction of this time. John's statement that he omitted many things from Jesus' life in making his book is evidently true of all the evangelists, and long gaps, such as are evident in the fourth gospel, must be assumed in the other three. Recalling the character of the gospels as portraits of Jesus rather than narratives of his life, we may easily acknowledge the incompleteness of the records of the three years of ministry.

Nevertheless, to effect such a change in conviction and feeling as Jesus wrought in the minds of his disciples required time. Three years are better suited to effect that change than one or two, and perhaps it took as many as four or five.

The apparent result of the first activity in the area of Jerusalem was disappointment, but not complete failure. Jesus had won a small cadre of adherents, but no considerable following in the capital. He had definitely excited the jealousy and opposition of the leading men of the nation. Even such popular enthusiasm as had followed his works was of a sort that Jesus could not encourage. The situation in Judea had finally become so nearly untenable that he decided to withdraw into seclusion in Galilee. He had gone to Jerusalem eager to begin there. Challenge, cold criticism, and superficial faith were the results. A new beginning needed to be made along other lines in other places. Therefore Jesus retreated to his home.

The work of Jesus in Galilee, the principal theme of the first three gospels, had begun with a move from Nazareth to Capernaum, and the calling of four fishermen to be his constant followers. The ready obedience which Simon and Andrew and James and John gave to this call is good evidence that they did not first come to know Jesus at the time of this summons. Possibly they were disciples of John the Baptist and knew Jesus then. The narrative presupposes some such earlier association as is reported in John, followed by a temporary return to their old homes and occupations, while Jesus sought seclusion after his work in Judea.

Although Matthew is the gospel giving the clearest general view of the work in Galilee, it lacks arrangement of details, and is not much help in determining the sequence of events. Jesus' first cures in the synagogue at Capernaum roused the interest and wonder of the multitudes to such an extent that he felt constrained to withdraw to other towns. On his return to Capernaum he was so beset with crowds that the friends of the paralytic could get at him only by breaking up the roof, which was no great problem since the roofs were lightly made of thatched materials.

It was when Jesus found himself followed by multitudes from all parts of the land that he selected twelve of his disciples "that they might be with him and that he might send them forth to preach," and addressed to them in the hearing of the multitudes the exacting, although unspeakably engaging teaching of the sermon on the mount. Things continued this way even after Herod Antipas had killed John the Baptist, for when Jesus, having heard of John's fate, sought retirement with his disciples across the Sea of Galilee, he was robbed of his seclusion by throngs who flocked to him to be healed and to hear of the kingdom of God.

At first Jesus impressed the people by his authoritative teaching and cures. After raising the widow's son at Nain, the popular feeling found a more definite declaration,—"a great prophet has risen up among us." The cure of a demoniac in Capernaum raised the further incredulous query, "Can this be the Son of David?" The notion that he might be the Messiah seems to have gained acceptance more and more as Jesus' popularity grew, for at the time of the feeding of the multitudes the enthusiasm burst into a flame of determination to force him to undertake the work for which he appeared to be so eminently fitted, but from which he fled ("Jesus, who could see they were about to come and take him by force and make him king, escaped back to the hills by himself," John 6:15).

Parallel with the growth of popular enthusiasm, and probably because of it, the religious leaders consistently maintained an attitude of opposition. The gospels connect the critics of Jesus now and again with the Pharisees of the capital, Jerusalem, while the Galilean Pharisees are represented as more or less friendly. At the first appearance of Jesus in Capernaum even the Sabbath cure in the synagogue passed unchallenged; but on the return from his first excursion to other towns, Jesus found critics in his audience (Luke connects them directly with Jerusalem). From time to time such censors as these objected to the forgiveness by Jesus of the sins of the paralytic (Mark 6:6-7), criticized his social relations with outcasts like the publicans (tax collectors, Mark 2:16), took offence at his carelessness of the Sabbath tradition in his instruction of his disciples (Mark 2:24), and sought to turn the tide of rising popular enthusiasm by ascribing his power to a pact with the devil (Mark 3:22). Baffled in one charge, they turned to another, until, after the feeding of the multitudes, Jesus showed his complete disregard of all they held most dear, replying to a criticism of his disciples for carelessness of the ritual of hand-washing by an authoritative setting aside of the whole body of their traditions, as well as of the laws of clean and unclean meats (Mark 7:1-23).

The curious thing is that although popular enthusiasm for Jesus was great, it was also reserved in its judgment about him. Galilee, the province which inspired a revolution during the early life of Jesus, and which furnished the chief support to the revolt against Rome a generation later, could have been excited to uncontrollable passion by the simple idea that a leader was present who could be made to head a movement for Jewish liberty. But there was something about Jesus which made it impossible to think of him as such a Messiah. He was much more moved by sin lurking within than by wrong inflicted from without. He looked for God's kingdom, but he looked for it within the heart more than in outward circumstances. Even those who were just as opposed as Jesus to any uprising against Rome found in Jesus something so contradictory of their idea of the celestial judge that they could not easily think of him as a Messiah. Jesus was a puzzle to the people. They were sure that he was a prophet; but if at any time some were tempted to query, "Can this be the Son of David?" the incredulous folk always expected a nega-

The Historical Perspective

tive reply.

In his teaching there was a simple claim of authority which indicates certainty on his part concerning his own mission. Yet the personal question of his divinity is so completely retired for the time, that in his rebuke of the blasphemy of the Pharisees he took pains to declare that it was not because they had spoken against the Son of Man that they were in danger, but because they had spoken against the Spirit of God, whose presence was manifest in his works.

Yet Jesus was not indifferent in Galilee to what the people thought about him. The question at Cæsarea Philippi shows more fully the aim of his ministry. During all the period of the preaching of the kingdom he never hesitated to assert himself whenever need for such self-assertion arose. This was evident in his dealing with the Pharisees. He rarely argued with them, and always assumed a tone of authority which was above challenge, asserting that the Son of Man had authority to forgive sins, was lord of the Sabbath, was greater than the Temple or Jonah or Solomon. Moreover, in his positive teaching of the new truth he assumed such an authoritative tone that his simple "I say unto you" left any who thought upon it wondering about the extraordinary claim of authority in that simple remark.

The key to the ministry in Galilee is furnished in Jesus' answer to the message from John the Baptist. John in prison had heard of the works of his successor. Jesus did so much that promised a fulfillment of the Messianic hope, yet left so much undone, contradicting in so many ways the current idea of a Messiah by his studied avoidance of any demonstration, that the older prophet, John the Baptist, felt a momentary doubt of the correctness of his earlier conviction. The question that John the Baptist asked was, "are you the one who is to come, or have we got to wait for someone else?" Jesus told the messenger. "Go back and tell John what you hear and see; the blind see again and the lame walk, lepers are cleansed, and the deaf hear, and the dead are raised to life and the Good News is proclaimed to the poor; and happy is the man who does not lose faith in me" (Matthew 11:2-6). It seems at first strange that John the Baptist experienced some doubt after that exalted moment of insight when he pointed out Jesus as the Lamb of God, but this can probably be explained by his distress and restless activity while caged within the walls of a prison. Jesus showed that he did not count it strange, by his treatment of John's question and by his words about John after the messengers had gone. Yet in his reply he gently suggested that the question already had its answer if John would but look rightly for it. He simply referred to the things that were being done before the eyes of all, and asked John to form from them a conclusion concerning the one who did them. And his answer was, in a manner of speaking, a coded reference to Isaiah: "Your dead will come to life (Isaiah 26:19), then the eyes of the blind shall be opened, the ears of the deaf unsealed (Isaiah 35:5-6), the spirit of the

The Historical Perspective

Lord Yahweh has been given to me, for Yahweh has anointed me. He has sent me to bring good news to the poor, to bind up hearts that are broken, to proclaim liberty to captives, freedom to those in prison (Isaiah 61:1)." Here Jesus emphasized his works, and allowed his message to speak for itself; but he frankly indicated that he expected people to pass from wonder at his ministry to an opinion about himself. At Cæsarea Philippi he showed to his disciples that this opinion about himself was the significant thing in his eyes.

Throughout the ministry in Galilee, therefore, this twofold aim appears. Jesus would first divert attention from himself to his message, in order that he might win disciples to the kingdom of God. Having so attached them to his idea of the kingdom, he desired to be recognized as that kingdom's prince, the Messiah promised by God for his people. He retired behind his message in order that men might be drawn to the truth which he held dear, knowing that thus they would find themselves led to him in a willing devotion.

This aim explains his retirement when popularity pressed, his exacting teaching about the spirituality of the kingdom of God, and his injunctions of silence. He wished to be known, to be thought about, to be accepted as God's anointed, but he would have this only by a genuine surrender to his leadership. His disciples must own him master and follow him, however much he might disappoint their misconceptions. This aim, too, explains his frank self-assertions and exalted personal claims in opposition to official criticism. He would not be false to his own sense of mission, nor allow people to think him bold when his critics were away, and cowardly in their presence. Therefore, when necessary, he invited attention to himself as greater than the Temple or as lord of the Sabbath. This kind of self-assertion, as well as his customary self-retirement, forced people to face the contradiction which he offered to the accepted religious ideas of their leaders.

The test of the personal attachment of the few came shortly after the execution of John the Baptist by Herod Antipas. Word of this tragedy was brought to Jesus by the Baptist's disciples about the time that he and the twelve returned to Capernaum from their tour of preaching. At the suggestion of Jesus they withdrew to the eastern side of the lake in search of rest. Such a desire for seclusion was intensified by the continued impetuous enthusiasm of the multitudes who flocked about him again in Capernaum. In fact, so insistent was their interest in Jesus that they would not allow him the quiet he sought, but followed around the lake in great numbers when they learned that he had crossed to the other side. He who came not to be ministered unto but to minister could not repel the crowds who came to him, and he at once "welcomed them, and spoke to them of the kingdom of God, and them that had need of healing he healed" (Luke 9:11). The day having passed in this ministry, he multiplied the small store of bread and fish brought by his disciples in order to feed the weary people. This work of power seemed to some among the multitudes to be the last thing needed to prove that Jesus was to be their promised deliverer, and they "were about to come and take him by force and make him king" (John 6:15), when he withdrew from them and spent the night in prayer.

This sudden determination on the part of the multitudes to force the hand of Jesus was probably due to the prevalence of the idea that the Messiah should feed his people, as Moses had provided them manna in the desert. The rebuff which Jesus quietly gave them did not cool their ardor, until on the following day, in the synagogue in Capernaum, he plainly taught them that they had quite missed the significance of his miracle. They thought of loaves and material sustenance. He would have had them find in these a sign that he could also supply their spiritual needs, and he insisted that this, and this alone, was his actual mission. From the very first, popular enthusiasm had had to ignore many contradictions of cherished notions. But his power and the indescribable force of his personality had served to hold them to a hope that Jesus would soon discard the perplexing role which he had chosen for the time to assume, and take up the proper work of the Messiah. This last refusal to accept what seemed to them to be his evident duty caused a revulsion in the popular feeling, and "many of his disciples turned back and walked no more with him" (John 6:66). The time of sifting had come. Jesus had known that such a rash determination to make him king was possible to the Galilean multitudes, and that whenever it should come it must be followed by disillusionment. Now the open ministry had run its course. As the multitudes were turning back and walking no more with him, he turned to the twelve with the question, "Will you also go away?" and found that with them his method had borne fruit. They clung to him in spite of disillusionment, for in him they had found what was better than their preconceptions.

It is John, the fourth gospel, which shows clearly the critical significance of this event. The others tell nothing of the sudden determination of the multitude, nor of the revulsion of feeling that followed Jesus' refusal to yield to their will. Yet these other gospels indicate in their narratives that from this time Jesus avoided the scenes of his former labors, and show that when from time to time he returned to the neighborhood of Capernaum he was met by such a spirit of hostility that he withdrew again immediately to regions where he and his disciples could have time for quiet discussion.

Outside the small group of Apostles, the months of toil in Galilee showed results hardly more significant than the grain of mustard seed or the little leaven. Popular enthusiasm had risen, increased, reached its climax, and waned. Official opposition had early been aroused, and had continued with a steadily deepened intensity. The wonderful teaching with authority, and the signs worked on those that were sick, had been as seed sown by the wayside or in thorny or in stony ground, except for the little handful who had felt the personal power of Jesus and had surrendered to it, ready to follow where he should lead, whether or not it should be in a path of their choice. This, however, was the proof that those months had actually been a time of rewarded toil.

With the crisis in Capernaum the ministry in Galilee may be said in one sense to have come to an end. Yet Jesus did not immediately go south to Jerusalem. Again he was found in or near Capernaum, with the time between these visits having been spent in regions to the north and northwest. The disciples were far from ready for the trial their loyalty was to meet before they had seen the end of the opposition to their Lord. The time intervening between the collapse of popularity and Jesus' final departure from Galilee may well be thought of as a time of further discipline of the faith of his followers and of added instruction concerning the truth for which their Master stood. The length of this supplementary period in Galilee is not definitely known. It extended from the Passover to about the Feast of Tabernacles (April to October). The record of what Jesus did and said in this time is meager, only enough being reported to show that it was a time of repeated withdrawals from Galilee and of private instruction for the disciples.

The disciples were trained in faith by further exhibitions of the complete break between their Master and the leaders of the people. This break appeared most clearly soon after the feeding of the multitudes in his reply to a criticism of the disciples for disregard of pharisaic traditions concerning handwashing (Mark 7:1-23). The critics insisted on the sacredness of their traditions. Jesus in reply scorned them for disregard of the plain demands of God's law, and freed men from bondage to the whole ritual of ceremonial cleanness and uncleanness, thus attacking Judaism in its citadel.

It was immediately after this, for reasons left unexplained, that he withdrew with his disciples to the regions of Tyre, a city on the coast in the territory of Syro-Phoenicia, north and west of Galilee. "While there, he went into a house and did not want anyone to know he was there." And it is assumed this was a Jewish household and that his purpose was to carry his message to the Jews living in that foreign area. But his fame had already spread far from the Jewish lands, and he was recognized by a woman who begged him to cure her daughter. His initial response was that he refused to "take the children's bread and cast it to the dogs" (Mark 7:27). But he had a change of heart, and cured the daughter.

It appears from his later attitude in the Gentile regions of the Decapolis, an area of Gentiles to the south and east of Galilee, that he no longer felt obliged to check his natural readiness to help the needy who sought him out while ministering to the Jews living in that area. Although in one instance, for reasons no longer known to us, Jesus charged a man whom he had cured to keep it secret (Mark 7:32 -37), in general his work in these heathen regions

seems, after the visit to Tyre, to have been quite un-
restrained, and to have produced the same enthusiasm that had earlier brought the multitudes to him
in Galilee, and it appears that his followers there
were both Jews and Gentiles

On his return a little later to the west side of the
sea of Galilee he was met by hostile Pharisees with a
demand for a sign, and after refusing to satisfy their
challenge, he and his disciples withdrew again from
Galilee towards Cæsarea Philippi. As they went on
their way, Jesus distinctly warned them against the
influence of their leaders, religious and political. So
far as our records tell us, Jesus returned only once
again to Capernaum. There he was met with the demand that he pay the Temple tax. This tax was usually collected just before the Passover. As this last
visit to Capernaum was probably not far from the
Feast of Tabernacles, Jesus seems to have been in
arrears. This may have been due to his absence from
Capernaum at the time of the collection. The prompt
answer of Peter may indicate that he knew that in
other years Jesus had paid this tax. The question,
however, implies official suspicion that Jesus was
seeking to evade payment, and exhibits further the
straining of the relations between him and the Jewish leaders.

Throughout the Holy Land the faith of the disciples had been constantly tested by the increasing opposition between Jesus and their old leaders. The
time would come when Jesus would send them forth
to make disciples of all the nations. But in the mean-

time, he made it his business to nurture their faith in him.

After the rebuff in Galilee, when the unbelieving Pharisees had again demanded a sign of his authority, and after he had definitely warned the disciples against the influence of their leaders, Jesus led his little company far to the north towards the slopes of Hermon, where he put them to the test. There, near the recently built city of Cæsarea Philippi, Jesus plainly asked his disciples what the people thought of him. He is told that the people look on him as a prophet, in whom the spirit of the men of old had been revived; but not a whisper remains of the former readiness to hail him as the Messiah. It was in the face of such a definite revulsion in the popular feeling, in the face, too, of the increasing hostility of all the great in the nation, that Peter answered for the twelve that they believed Jesus to be the Messiah. Jesus immediately declared that the faith that could answer thus could spring only from a heavenly source.

One after another the Apostles' ideas of how a Messiah should act and what he should be had been contradicted in what Jesus was and did. Yet after the weeks of withdrawal from Galilee, Peter could only in effect assert anew what he had declared at Capernaum—that Jesus had the words of eternal life. In his commendation of Peter, Jesus revealed the secret of his method in the work which, because of this confession, he could now proceed to do more rapidly. He cuts loose utterly from the method of the scribes. He, the new teacher, commits to them no body of teaching which they are to give to others as the key to eternal life. The salvation they are to preach is a salvation by personal attachment; that is, by faith alone. The rock on which he will build his church is personal attachment, faith that is ready to leave all and follow him.

Peter was to be the cornerstone of that faith that is ready to leave all, a faith whose very nature it is to be contagious, and associate with itself others of "like precious faith." Peter's faith was as yet meager, as he showed at once; but it was a genuine surrender of his heart to his Lord's guidance and control. This was the distinctive mark of the new religious life inaugurated by Jesus of Nazareth.

If anything were needed to prove that the idea that he was the Messiah was no new thought to Jesus, it could be found in the lesson which he at once began to teach his disciples. The confession of Peter indicated to him simply that the first stage in his work had been completed. He immediately began to prepare the disciples for the end which for some time past he had seen to be inevitable. He taught them more than that his death was inevitable; he declared that it was divinely necessary that he should be put to death as a result of the hostility of the Jews to him ("the Son of Man must suffer"). All the contradictions which he had offered to the Messianic ideas of his disciples paled into insignificance beside this one. When they saw how he failed to meet the hopes that were commonly held, they needed only to remember to be patient, expecting that in time he would cast off the strange mask and take to himself his power and reign. But it was too much for the late confessed and very genuine faith of Peter to hear that the Messiah must die. So unthinkable was the idea, that Peter assumed that Jesus had become unduly discouraged by the relentlessness of the opposition which had driven him first out of Judea and later out of Galilee. Accordingly Peter sought to turn his Master's mind to a brighter prospect, asserting that his forebodings could not be true. It is hard for us to conceive the chill of heart which must have followed the glow of his confession when he heard the stern rebuke of Jesus, who found in Peter's last words the voice of the Evil One, as before in his confession he had recognized the Spirit of God.

It was possibly at this time, certainly near the end of the Galilean ministry, that Jesus was approached by his own brothers, who urged him to try to win the capital. Their attitude was not one of indifference, though clearly not one of actual faith in his claim. "As the Jewish Feast of Tabernacles drew near, his brothers said to him, 'Why not leave this place and go to Judea, and let your disciples [those in Jerusalem and Judea] see the works you are doing," (John 7:2-5). It seems at this point his brothers, possibly James and Jude, were involved in his ministry and felt that Jesus had not made adequate effort to secure a following in Jerusalem, and that he could not hope for success in his work if he continued to confine his attention to Galilee. Jesus knew condi-

The Historical Perspective

tions in Jerusalem far better than they did, and had no desire as yet of resuming a general ministry there. He therefore dismissed the suggestion, and told his brothers to go up to the feast without him.

Yet Jesus still yearned over Jerusalem. There were some in the capital who had real faith in him. His repeated efforts to win Jerusalem mean nothing if we do not recognize that he hoped against hope that other people might yet turn and let him lead them. With some such purpose, he went up a little later without ostentation, and quietly appeared in the Temple teaching. The effect of this unannounced arrival was that the opposition was not ready for him. This resulted in a division of sentiment among the people, so much so that when the leaders, both secular and religious, sought to achieve his arrest, the officers sent to take Jesus were themselves entranced by his teaching. In spite of the wish of the leaders, Jesus continued to teach, and many of the people began to think favorably of him. When, however, he tried to lead them on to become "disciples indeed," they took offence, and showed that they were not ready to follow him.

Upon his earlier departure from Galilee for Jerusalem for the Feast of Tabernacles, it appears that Jesus started southward through Samaria, and sent out the seventy "into every city and place where he himself was about to come." It is impossible to determine where the seventy were sent. The "towns and cities" where Jesus was about to come may have included some from all portions of the land, not excepting Judea.

John is silent concerning the doings of Jesus after the Feast of Tabernacles. In 10:22 he notes that Jesus was at Jerusalem at the Feast of Dedication, which followed two months later. The Feast of Tabernacles, known as Sukkot in the Jewish religion, begins on the 15th day of the month of Tishrei (late September to late October). It is one of the three biblically mandated festivals during which Jews were commanded to make a pilgrimage to the Temple in Jerusalem. The holiday lasts seven days. The Hebrew word sukkōt is the plural of sukkah, " tabernacle", which is a walled structure covered with palm leaves. The sukkah is intended as a reminiscence of the fragile dwellings in which the Israelites dwelt during their 40 years of travel in the desert after the Exodus. Throughout the holiday meals are eaten inside the sukkah and many sleep there as well (Sukkot - Jewish Virtual Library). The Feast of Dedication also called "Feast of the Maccabees" was a Jewish festival observed for eight days from the 25th of Kislev according to the Hebrew calendar, which may occur at any time from late November to late December in the Gregorian calendar. It was instituted by Judas Maccabeus, who won independence for Israel, in the year 165 BC in commemoration of the reconsecration of the Temple. During the festival, houses and synagogues were illuminated and Psalm 30, a thanksgiving after mortal danger, is recited. In modern Jewish practice, the festival is known as Hanukah, and the festival is observed by the kindling of the lights of the nine-branched Menorah.

It seems probable that after his hurried and private journey to the Feast of Tabernacles, Jesus returned to Galilee and gathered to himself again the little company of his loyal followers, in preparation for that final journey to Jerusalem.

The fourth gospel, John, says that after this second visit to Jerusalem, at the Feast of Dedication (Hanukah), Jesus went back again to the far side of the Jordan to the place where John the Baptist had been baptizing at the first (10:40). Matthew and Mark also say that in this region the multitudes again flocked to him, and he resumed his ministry of teaching.

From there, Jesus hastened, at the summons of his friends, to Bethany when Lazarus died. It is not strange that the disciples feared this third return to Judea, nor that Jesus did not hesitate when he recognized the call of duty as well as of friendship. In no recorded miracle of Jesus is his power more signally set forth, yet here more clearly than anywhere else he is represented as dependent on his Father in his exercise of that power. The words of Jesus at the grave show that he was confident of the resurrection of Lazarus, because he had prayed and was sure he was heard. It may be that his delay after hearing of the sickness of his friend was a time of waiting for answer, and that this explains his confidence of safety when the time came for him to expose himself again to the hostility of Judea.

The effect of the resurrection of Lazarus was such
as to intensify the determination of the leaders in Jerusalem—both Pharisees and Sadducees—to get rid
of Jesus as dangerous to the quiet of the nation
(John 11:47-54). Caiaphas, the high priest that year,
said, "You don't seem to have grasped the situation
at all; you fail to see that it is better for one man to
die for the people, than for the whole nation to be destroyed." Thus, it is clear that the ruling class of
Jews were concerned that Jesus could well be the
leader of a revolt that would bring in the Roman
troops who would destroy the Temple and the city.
The reported raising of Lazarus does not appear in
John as the sole cause of the arrest of Jesus, but
rather as one of the factors leading to it. It was the
total contradiction by Jesus of so many current and
cherished ideas that led to his condemnation; the
raising of Lazarus only showed that he was becom-
ing dangerously popular, and made the priestly leaders feel the necessity of haste. The silence of the first
three gospels concerning this event is truly perplexing, yet it is not any more difficult to explain than
the silence of all four evangelists concerning the appearance of the risen Jesus to James, or to the five
hundred brethren. Room must be allowed in our conception of the life of Jesus for many incidents to
which only one of the gospels is witness. Moreover,
after the collapse of popularity in Galilee, the great
enthusiasm of the multitudes over Jesus when he entered Jerusalem is most easily understood if he had
made some such manifestation of power as the resto-

The Historical Perspective

ration of Lazarus.

After the visit to Bethany, his third trip to Judea that season, Jesus withdrew to a little town named Ephraim, on the border between Judea and Samaria, and spent some time there in seclusion with his disciples, doubtless strengthening his personal hold on them in preparation for the shock their faith was about to receive. Of the length of this sojourn nothing is told us, nor of the road by which Jesus left Ephraim for Jerusalem. The first three gospels show that he began his final approach to the Holy City at Jericho (Mark 10:46). It may be that he descended from Ephraim direct to Jericho some days before the Passover, rejoining there some of the people who had been impressed by his recent ministry in the region "where John at the first was baptizing."

It is natural to suppose that it was on this journey to Jericho that he warned his disciples again of the fate which he saw before him in Jerusalem, and quite probably it was at this time that he rebuked the crude ambition of the sons of Zebedee by reminding them that his disciples must be more ambitious to serve than to rule, since even "the Son of Man came not to be ministered unto but to minister, and to give his life as a ransom for many" (Mark 10:35-45). At Jericho he was at once crowded upon by enthusiastic multitudes.

This enthusiasm received a shock when Jesus chose to be the guest of a chief of the publicans in Jericho (the principal tax collector who contracted directly with the Romans), a shock which Jesus probably intended, for much the same reason that led him afterwards to teach his followers, in the parable of the pounds, that they must be ready for a long delay in his actual assumption of his kingly right. Finally, six days before the Passover, he and his disciples left Jericho and went up to Bethany again, preparatory to his final appearance in Jerusalem.

CHAPTER 10

The Last Days of Jesus
by
Benjamin Rush Rhees
Edited and supplemented by Charles
Daudert

It is probable that the caravan with which Jesus was traveling reached Bethany not long before the sunset which marked the beginning of the Sabbath preceding the Passover. Jesus had friends there, and the Sabbath was doubtless spent quietly in this retreat. The general cordiality of the welcome expressed itself in a feast given in the house of one Simon, a leper who had probably experienced the power of Jesus to heal. He may have been a relative of Lazarus, for Martha assisted in the entertainment, and Lazarus was one of the guests of honor. During the feast, Mary, the sister of Lazarus, poured forth on the head and feet of Jesus a box of the rarest perfume.

The day following the supper at Bethany, Palm Sunday, the first day of the week, witnessed the welcome of Jesus to Jerusalem by the jubilant multitudes.

His mode of entering the city was in marked contrast to his flight from those determined to make him king after he had fed the multitudes in Galilee. In some respects the circumstances were similar. A multitude of the visitors to the feast, hearing that Jesus was at Bethany on his way to Jerusalem, went out to meet him with a welcome that showed their enthusiastic confidence that at last he would assume Messianic power and redeem Israel. Jesus was now ready for a popular demonstration, because the rulers were no longer willing to tolerate his work and his teaching. He had never hesitated to assert his superiority to official criticism, and at length the hour had come to proclaim the full significance of his independence. In fact it was for this reason that some months before he had steadfastly determined to go to Jerusalem.

When the crowd from Jerusalem appeared, Jesus took the initiative in a genuine Messianic demonstration. He sent two of his disciples to a place near by to borrow an ass's colt, on which he might ride into the city, fulfilling Zechariah's prophecy of the "king that comes meekly, and riding upon an ass" (see Matthew 21:4-5). At this, the enthusiasm of his followers, and of those who had come to meet him, became unbounded, and without rebuke from Jesus they proceeded towards Jerusalem crying, "Hosanna; Blessed is he that comes in the name of the Lord" (Mark 11:9-10). Notwithstanding the remonstrances of certain friendly Pharisees among the multitude, Jesus accepted the hosannas, for they served to emphasize the claim which he now wished, without reserve or ambiguity, to make in Jerusalem.

The Historical Perspective

The time for reserve had passed. The mass of the people with their leaders had shown clearly that they had no liking for his truth or himself as bearer of it; while the few had become sufficiently attached to him to warrant the supreme test of their faith. He could not continue his efforts to win the people, for both Galilee and Judea were closed to him, and Herod Antipas had already been regarding him with suspicion.

For the last encounter he entered the city as its promised deliverer, the Prince of Peace. The very method of his Messianic proclamation was a challenge of current Jewish ideas, for they were not looking for so meek and peaceful a leader as Zechariah had conceived; this entrance emphasized the old contradiction between Jesus and his people's expectations.

On the following day Jesus furnished to his disciples a parable in action, illustrating the fate that awaited the nation; for it is only as a parable that the curse of the barren fig-tree can be understood. He was drawn to it by the early foliage, for it was not yet the season for either fruit or leaves. The withering of the fig-tree set his disciples thinking; and Jesus showed that it was an object lesson, promising that the disciples, by the exercise of but a little faith, could do more, even move mountains.

The curse upon the barren fig-tree was spoken as Jesus was going from Bethany to Jerusalem on the morning after his Messianic entry, that is, on Monday, and it was on Monday Jesus entered into the

Temple and taught and healed. It is at this point that Mark inserts the cleansing of the Temple which John shows to belong rather to Jesus' first public visit to Jerusalem years earlier. The place which this incident holds in the first three gospels has already been explained by the fact that it furnished one cause for the official hostility to Jesus, and that Mark's story included no earlier visit to the holy city.

Tuesday, the last day of public activity, shows Jesus in four different lights, how he dealt with his critics, with the devout widow, with the inquiring Greeks, and with his own disciples.

The opposition to him expressed itself, after the general challenge of his authority, in three questions put in succession by Pharisees and *Herodians, by Sadducees, and by a scribe, more earnest than most, whom the Pharisees put forward after they had seen how Jesus silenced the Sadducees. Jesus met the opening challenge by a question about John's baptism which completely destroyed the complacency of his critics, putting them on the defensive.

[*Note: The Herodians were a sect or party mentioned as having on two occasions—once in Galilee and again in Jerusalem—manifested an unfriendly disposition towards Jesus (Mark 3:6, 12:13; Matthew 22:16; cf. also Mark 8:15, Luke 13:31-32, Acts 4:27). The Herodians were likely a political party which supported Herod Antipas, the son of Herod the Great]

The Historical Perspective

In none of his words had Jesus so clearly asserted the simple other-worldliness of his doctrine of the kingdom of God as in his answer to the question about tribute (render unto Caesar what is Caesar's and unto God what is God's). For him loyalty to the actual earthly sovereign was quite compatible with loyalty to God.

A second assault was made by some Sadducees who put to him a crude question about the relations of a several-times married woman in the resurrection. If this question were asked with the expectation of making Jesus ridiculous in the sight of the people it was a marked failure, for his reply was so simple and straightforward that he won the admiration even of some of the Pharisees. The next test was more purely academic in character—as to what class of commands is greatest in the law. For the pharisaic scholars this was a favorite problem. For Jesus, however, the question contained no problem, since all the law is summed up in the two commandments of love. The Pharisees immediately saw the truth of his generalization, and, in this last attack, were moved with admiration for the fineness and sufficiency of Jesus' answer.

Never have sharper words of reproach fallen upon human ears than those which Jesus directed against the scribes and Pharisees; they are burdened with indignation for the misleading of the people, with rebuke for the misrepresentation of God's truth, and with scorn for their hollow pretence of righteousness. The change of scene which introduces the widow offering her gift in the Temple treasury heightens the significance of the controversies through which Jesus had just passed. In his comment on the worth of her two mites we hear again the preacher of the Sermon on the Mount. There is again a reference to the insight of him who sees in secret, and who judges as he sees; while allusion is not lacking to the others whose larger gifts attracted a wider attention.

Still a different side of Jesus appears when the Greeks seek him in the Temple. Having visited Jerusalem for the feast, they heard on every hand about the new teacher. They were not so bound to rabbinic traditions as the Jews themselves. They had been drawn by the finer features of Judaism—its high morality and its noble idea of God, and most significantly, the theology of monotheism. What they heard of Jesus might well attract them, and they sought out Philip, a disciple with a Greek name, to request an interview with his Master. The effect of their seeking Jesus was marked, for it offered sharp contrast to the rejection he now felt in his dealings with the people, who but two days before had hailed him as Messiah.

In all the earlier events of the day the disciples of Jesus seldom appear. He is occupied with others, accepting the challenge of the leaders, and completing his testimony to the truth they refused to hear. The quieter hours of the later part of the day gave time for further words with his friends. The comment on the widow's gift was meant for them, and the uncovering of his own soul when the Greeks sought him

The Historical Perspective

was in their presence. After he had left the Temple and the city he turned to them more exclusively. His disciples were perplexed by what they saw and felt, for the temper of the people toward their Master could not be mistaken. Yet they were sure of him. The disciples asked him to say when the catastrophe, to which he had made repeated reference during the day, should take place. The conversation which followed is reported for us in the discourse on the destruction of Jerusalem and the end of the world (Mark 13 and parallels), in which Jesus taught his disciples to expect trouble in their ministry, as he was meeting trouble in his.

With this the curtain falls on the public ministry of Jesus. On Thursday Jesus and his disciples returned to Jerusalem for the last time. Knowing the temper of the leaders, and the danger of arrest at any time, Jesus was particularly eager to eat the Passover with his disciples, and he sent two of them—Luke names them as Peter and John—to prepare for the supper. He directed them carefully how to find the house where a friend would provide them the upper room that was needed for an undisturbed meeting of the little band, and the two went on in advance to make ready. When the hour came, Jesus with the others went to the appointed place and sat down for the supper.

Luke and John give the most complete reports of what was said at the table. All the gospels tell of Peter's declaration of superior loyalty and the prediction of his threefold denial; Luke, however, adds that in connection with it, Jesus assured Peter of his restoration, and charged him to strengthen his brethren. John alone gives the long and full discourse of admonition and comfort, followed by Jesus' prayer for his disciples. It is evident from the words of Jesus as he entered the garden of Gethsemane (Mark 14:33 -34), that his heart had been greatly troubled during the supper.

He realized that the approaching separation would sorely try the faith of his followers, and he sought to strengthen them by showing his own calmness in view of it. He urged them to maintain their devotion to him, and to seek and find the source of their life and strength in fellowship with him—who would always be present, though unseen among them. He sought to convince them that his departure was to be for their advantage, that fellowship with him spiritually would be far more real and meaningful than what they had already experienced.

How long the conversation continued, or when the company left the upper chamber, cannot be told. At some time before the arrival at Gethsemane, Jesus turned to God in prayer for the disciples whom he was about to leave to the severe trial of their faith, asking for them that realization of eternal life which he had enjoyed and exemplified in his own intimate life with his Father.

Of the garden of Gethsemane it is only known that it was across the Kidron, on the slope of the Mount of Olives. Tradition has long pointed to an enclosure some fifty yards beyond the bridge that crosses the ravine on the road leading eastward from St. Stephen's gate. Most students feel that this is too near the city and the highway for the place of retreat chosen by Jesus. It is enough to know that in some olive grove on the mountainside, where an oil-press gave a name to the place (Gethsemane), Jesus withdrew with his disciples on that last night.

The band that arrested Jesus was accompanied by a few Roman auxiliaries from the garrison of the city, but they were not needed. The disciples offered no appreciable resistance; on the contrary, "they all forsook him and fled" (Mark 14:50). Having arrested Jesus, the band took him to Annas, the actual leader of Jewish affairs, though not at the time the official high-priest. He had held that office some time before, as stated earlier, but had been deposed by the Roman governor of Syria after being in power for nine years. His influence continued, however, for although he was never reinstated, he seems to have been able to secure the appointment for members of his own family during a period of many years. Caiaphas, the legal high-priest, was his son-in-law. Annas, as the leader of aristocratic opinion in Jerusalem, had doubtless been foremost in the secret counsels which led to the decision to get rid of Jesus, hence the captive was, as a matter of course, taken first to his house.

Proceedings before the Jewish authorities were irregular. There seems to have been an informal examination of Jesus and various witnesses, first before Annas, and then before Caiaphas and a group of members of the Sanhedrin, the outcome of which was complete failure to secure evidence against Jesus from their false witnesses, and the formulation of a charge of blasphemy in consequence of his answer to the high-priest acknowledging himself to be the Messiah. The early morning hours were given over to mockery and abuse of the captive Jesus. When morning came, the Sanhedrin was convened, and he was condemned to death on the charge of blasphemy, and then led in bonds to the Roman governor for execution, since the Romans had taken from the Sanhedrin the authority to execute a death sentence. Before Pilate, the Jews had to name an offence recognized by Roman law; his accusers therefore falsified his claim and made him out a political Messiah, hostile to Roman rule. Pilate soon saw that the charge was trumped up, and sought in every way, while keeping the good-will of the people, to escape the responsibility of giving sentence against Jesus. His first effort was a simple declaration that he found no fault in the prisoner. Then, having heard that he was a Galilean, he tried to transfer the case to Herod Antipas, who happened to be in the city at the time. After that, he sought to compromise by agreeing to chastise Jesus and then release him. Next he offered the people their choice between the innocent Jesus and Barabbas, a convicted insurrectionist. The people, instructed by the priests, chose Barabbas, caring nothing for a Messiah who would allow himself to be arrested without resistance. That the populace so easily changed their cry from "hosanna" to "crucify him" is not surprising. Their hosannas were due to a complete misconception of Jesus' aim and purpose; disappointed in him, they would be the first to cry out against him, especially when the choice was between Jesus and a "real" insurrectionist.

CHAPTER 11

The Crucifixion

Crucifixion is the most brutal and painful method of execution humanity could possibly contrive. It can be described only as excruciating, a word derived from crucifixion, and which literally means "out of (ex) crucifying." Death was particularly slow and painful; the procedure was gruesome, and publically humiliating. The crucifixion of Jesus has been so sanitized and glossed over that one is hardly aware of the enormous cruelty and suffering endured by him upon the cross. He is depicted as wearing a loin cloth so as not to disturb the sensibilities of modern societies. And although he could have been crucified fully clothed, that was not the object. The purpose was public humiliation of the victim. The victim was on public display, naked, forced to urinate and defecate in full view of all.

It appears to be commonly believed that the Jews killed Jesus. Whether or not this conception arises out of the case that the gospels were written mainly in Greek primarily for consumption by gentiles, and with an eye toward placating the Romans, is immaterial. The simple facts are that the Jewish population did not crucify Jesus, the Romans, at the bidding of their Jewish puppet rulers, did. The act of

The Historical Perspective

crucifixion was forbidden by Jewish law, and execution was normally by stoning, and possibly by burning, perhaps even strangulation, or decapitation. The imposition of the death sentence had been taken away from the Jews and reserved to Rome, therefore it was to the Romans that the Jewish elite turned.

Jesus was singled out for extraordinary measures. He was subjected to scourging, and methodically beaten over his entire body with implements especially designed for the purpose. And it was not the Jews who did this, but the Roman soldiers. Pilate had hoped that he could avoid crucifixion by satisfying the leaders of the Sanhedrin with a thorough scourging. But the troops were so thorough and systematic in their task that Jesus was unable to carry his cross beam because of weakness from severe bleeding, which more than likely resulted in his death prior to expiration of the two criminals crucified with him. Nor was it the Jews who forced a crown of thorns down upon his head. We must also remember that it was the thorns forced into his scalp which kept the crown in place and which caused further bleeding. Nor was it the Jews who nailed the wooden sign over his head, proclaiming him "King of the Jews," nor was it the Jews who mocked him upon the cross. The gospels tell us that Pilate's real purpose was to avoid crucifixion by such severe treatment. Pilate also felt that perhaps he could win sympathy for Jesus and that the Jews might relent. However laudable those claims might be, the result was such a complete destruction of Jesus that he was likely near death before he was ever nailed to the cross.

It was always the Romans who executed by crucifixion. Their victims were left on display as warnings to others who might attempt dissent. To achieve that purpose, the sites of crucifixions were along public ways. The bodies were left there to rot and decompose, or until consumed by animals and carrion. And it was not a pleasant sight.

The legs of the victim were broken or shattered with an iron club, which not only hastened the death of the person, but was also meant to deter others from committing similar crimes or acts of disobedience. A further reason was to bring an end to the day's activities, since the Roman soldiers were obliged to remain on post until the victim died, and none of them were especially anxious to remain until after dark. The criminals executed with Jesus were subjected to this further painful procedure, which did result in their death shortly afterward. But Jesus had already died because of his weakened condition, and his death was confirmed by a spear thrust into his side.

The causes of death upon the cross were multiple. Nails were pounded through the wrists, as the palm may not have been sufficient to support the weight of the victim. The victim's feet were fastened to the cross by nails through the ankle or heel bone. In 1968, archaeologists discovered the remains of one Jehohanan, who had been crucified at about the same time as was Jesus. The remains included a heel bone with a nail driven through it from the side, which indicates that in the case of crucifixion, the heels were nailed to opposite sides of the post. Apparently, the purpose of nailing the feet to the cross was to provide leverage so that the victim could help support his body with his legs, prolonging his death, which might occur sooner because of difficulty breathing if supported only by his arms. Breaking the legs later in the day finally accomplished that result. In some cases, the shock and extreme pain of nails driven through the palms or wrists, and through the ankles or heel bones would, by itself, be sufficient to cause death. There would also be severe bleeding from the wounds to the hands and feet, bleeding which would be continually aggravated by enlargement of the wounds as the victim twisted and turned upon the cross, involuntary movements which could not be prevented because of the excruciating pain.

If the victim did not die from shock or loss of blood, death would finally come through dehydration or asphyxiation. When exhausted and no longer able to hold himself up on the cross, the victim would have great difficulty inhaling because of the forces on the chest muscles, and could die within a few minutes. When the legs were finally broken, death usually followed almost immediately through severe traumatic shock and eventual asphyxiation.

And that is how Jesus of Nazareth died upon the cross, an agonizing, prolonged death by crucifixion. Near the cross stood his mother and his mother's sister, and perhaps one disciple (John 19:25-27). Although Peter had witnessed his hearing before the Sanhedrin and his trial before Pontius Pilate, there is no evidence that Peter was present at the crucifixion. Along with the other disciples, he had gone into hiding. Nor is there any evidence that the brothers of Jesus were there, although they were probably in Jerusalem for the Passover. That is why Jesus entrusted to the disciple who was there, most probably John, someone closer to him than his brothers, the care of his mother, Mary.

Joseph of Arimathea, himself a member of the Sanhedrin, obtained from Pilate permission to take the body of Jesus down from the cross, which he and Nicodemus did, wrapping the body in linen cloth and placing it in a tomb belonging to Joseph of Arimathea, not far from the site of the crucifixion. Joseph and Nicodemus were secret disciples of Jesus, and may have been the two Pharisees who had come to tell Jesus that he should flee because Herod Antipas planned to have him killed.

The women returned to the tomb in the dark of the following Sunday morning, and saw that the stone had been rolled away and the tomb was empty, and the world has never been the same since.

CHAPTER 12

The Risen Christ

1. THE RESURRECTION

The early Christians were greatly interested in the teachings of Jesus and in his deeds, but they treasured most his resurrection, the victory he won out of seeming defeat. This is established by the fact that over one third of the first two gospels (Matthew and Mark), over one-fifth of Luke, and nearly one-half of John are devoted to the story of the passion and resurrection. This is not strange in view of the shock which the death of Jesus caused his disciples, and then the renewal which the resurrection brought to their hearts. The resurrection was the fundamental theme of apostolic preaching, the supreme evidence that Jesus was the Messiah.

A general view of the events of that third day after his crucifixion and those which followed can be constructed from our gospels and Paul. Early on the first day of the week (Sunday) Mary Magdalene, Mary the mother of James and Joseph, Salome, and others, came to anoint the body of Jesus. They found that the stone had been rolled back from the tomb. Mary Magdalene ran to tell Peter and John. The others saw a vision of angels which said that Jesus was alive and would see his disciples in Galilee, and ran to report this to the disciples. Meanwhile Mary Magdalene returned, following Peter and John who ran to see the tomb, and found it empty as she had said. She lingered after they left, and Jesus appeared to her, she mistaking him at first for the gardener. She then went to tell the disciples that she had seen the Lord. These events evidently occurred in the early morning.

One of the next incidents reported is that of the walk of two disciples to Emmaus, and the appearance of Jesus to them. At first they did not recognize him, not even when he taught them out of the scriptures the necessity that the Messiah should die. He was made known when at evening he sat down with them to a meal. This is the first manifestation reported by Paul, although probably before this event Jesus had appeared to Peter. Luke 24:12 tells us that when the two to whom Jesus had appeared on the road to Emmaus again reached Jerusalem the disciples received them with the news that Peter had seen the Lord. That same evening Jesus appeared suddenly among the disciples in their well-guarded upper room. His coming was such that he had to convince the disciples that he was not simply a disembodied spirit. Luke says that he did this by bidding them handle him, and by eating part of a fish before them. According to John, Thomas was not with the others at this first meeting with the disciples. A week later, presumably in Jerusalem, Jesus again manifested himself to the little company, Thomas being with them, and Jesus dispelling the doubt of that disciple.

The next appearance was probably to the seven

disciples by the Sea of Galilee, when Peter, who had denied three times, was then tested three times concerning his love for his Lord. After that followed the meeting on the mountain reported in Matthew, which was probably the same as the appearance to the five hundred. Next, probably still in Galilee, Jesus appeared to his brother James, who from that time on was a leader among the disciples. The next manifestation recorded was the final one in Jerusalem, after which Jesus led his disciples out as far as Bethany and was separated from them, henceforth to be thought of by them as seated at the right hand of God.

2. BARABBAS

Jesus (Hebrew Joshua) was a common name, which meant "Yahweh is salvation" (Catholic Encyclopedia: Origin of the name Jesus Christ), and was given to many sons by hopeful parents. In Luke 1:26-33, the angel Gabriel tells Mary to name the child "Jesus", and in Matthew 1:21 an angel tells Joseph "you are to name the child Jesus because he will save his people from their sins."

Jesus and his followers from Galilee spoke a dialect of Aramaic which was immediately recognized by the local population and set them aside as being foreign to the area of Jerusalem. In reporting Peter's denials, Matthew tells us that one of the bystanders came up and said to Peter, "You are one of them for sure! Why, your accent gives you away."

On the morning of the crucifixion, Pilate presented to the assembled masses two men, one of whom at Passover was to be freed by tradition. He asked them to make a choice between the local man who had started a riot and instigated open revolt against Rome, and the man from Galilee he knew was innocent of the charge of sedition. One can well imagine the confusion among the assembled masses who had heard the rumors that a miracle-worker named Jesus was among them and was to be crucified that day. When Pilate asked them which man shall be set free, Jesus bar Abbas (Jesus the Son of the Father), a local boy, or this Jesus from Galilee, the one with the foreign accent whose followers were in hiding, they naturally turned to the chief priests for guidance. The chief priests, serving at the pleasure of Rome, told them to choose Jesus bar Abbas, shortened to Barabbas in Mathew (Matthew 27:20-26), which they did. And this choice, which can be just as easily charged to a case of intentional misrepresentation on the part of the authorities, has been a source of anti-Semitism throughout the centuries since. Additionally, as is pointed out later, the Jewish leadership and high priests were puppets of Rome and did not represent the masses, therefore, the Jews, as a people, should never be blamed for the death of Jesus. This is clearly best illustrated by the fact that when the Jews finally did revolt against Rome, one of the first to be assassinated by the Jews was the high priest.

CHAPTER 13

The Early Church

It is fair to say that, aside from the New Testament, all we know of the early Christian Church during the first century comes from Josephus and the brief accounts given by Tacitus, Suetonius and Pliny the Younger. The next major historian to aid us in an understanding of the early church is Eusebius of Caesarea (263-339 CE). Eusebius was a Christian historian, and he became the Bishop of Caesarea in Palestine about the year 314. He was a scholar of the Biblical cannon, and was known as the "Father of Church History." He wrote the *Ecclesiastical History*, a rich source of Christian tradition. He also wrote many other works, most of which have been lost, but his *Ecclesiastical History* has survived primarily intact. It is a chronological account, based on earlier sources, complete from the period of the Apostles down to his own time. His chronology correlated the history of the Roman Empire with the history of the Church. Included were the bishops and other teachers of the Church, Christian relations with the Jews, the heretics, and the martyrs.

Eusebius was born into the Christian community at Caesarea, which at that time had a population of around 100,000. It had been a city of gentiles since Pompey conquered Judea, although it did have a large Jewish and Samaritan minority. Caesarea was a center of Christian theology. Eusebius was a student of the Christian school there, which had a large and valuable library of original manuscripts, including several Bibles from all parts of the world.

The *Ecclesiastical History* was finished by Eusebius sometime prior to the year 300. At about the same time, Eusebius worked on his *Chronicle*, a calendar of events from the time of creation, which correlated with his history of the Church. The great controversy at the time revolved around concepts of the Trinity. Eusebius supported the view of Arius, who taught the subordination of the Son to the Father. Although on the wrong side of the theology of the Trinity, Eusebius survived because he gained the favor of Emperor Constantine. This was probably because Eusebius was working on the biography of the emperor at that time. The biography was not completed, however, until after Constantine's death in 337 AD. However, Constantine knew of the work and had been consulted many times prior to his death. Eusebius died two years later.

As we know from the New Testament, the first Christians were ethnic Jews. Jesus preached to the Jewish people, and it was from them that he called forth his first disciples. The first and best history of the Church after the crucifixion is *The Acts of the Apostles*, written by Luke. Luke, a doctor, was a Syrian from Antioch. Paul described him as a close friend who stayed by him during his two periods of captivity in Rome. Luke probably also accompanied Paul on his second and third missions. Acts ends with Paul's second captivity in Rome (61-63 AD).

The Historical Perspective

From the accounts of Tacitus, we know that beginning with the year 64 AD, large scale persecutions of the Christians by authorities of the Roman Empire followed. It was the year that Nero blamed the Christians for the great fire of Rome. And it was under Nero, according to church tradition, that Peter and Paul were martyred in Rome. For the next 250 years Christians suffered sporadic persecutions, primarily for their refusal to worship the Roman Emperor as a god, which was considered to be treason, punishable by execution.

Finally, Galerius, a Roman Emperor who had previously been one of the leading figures in the persecution of Christians, issued an edict in 311 AD which ended the opposition to Christianity. It appears that Galerius was a humanitarian, who was appalled at the mass killings which became necessary to restrain the Christian movement. His decision was also a practical one, as the Christian population had exploded. They were everywhere, in great numbers, and there was no longer any reasonably expedient method of containing them.

Galerius was succeeded by Constantine the Great, who may have been under the influence of his mother, Helena, a devout Christian. At the Battle of Milvian Bridge (the bridge over the Tiber in northern Rome) in 312 AD, Constantine ordered his troops to adorn their shields with the Christian symbol, a vision that he had had the night before. After winning that battle, Constantine supported the Church financially, built various basilicas, granted privileges (e.g., exemption from certain taxes) to clergy, promoted Christians to some high ranking offices, and returned property confiscated during the Great Persecution of Diocletian, the emperor prior to Galerius. Between the years 324 and 330, Constantine built a completely new imperial capital that came to be named for him: Constantinople, which is now known as Istanbul. It had Christian architecture, contained churches within the city walls, and had no pagan temples. Christianity was secure. In 325 Constantine summoned the Council of Nicaea, which issued the Nicene Creed. Among other things, the Nicene Creed professed a belief in "One Holy Catholic Apostolic Church." Constantine had established a precedent for the emperor as responsible to God for the spiritual health of his subjects, and with a duty to maintain orthodoxy. The emperor was to enforce doctrine, root out heresy, and uphold ecclesiastical unity.

On February 27, 380, Theodosius I, then Roman Emperor, issued the Edict of Thessalonica, and the Roman Empire officially adopted Trinitarian Christianity as the state religion. After that, the Church adopted the same organizational boundaries as the empire, dioceses, being territorial divisions. The bishop of Rome was still held to be the "First among equals," and the bishop of Constantinople was second in precedence at the new capital of the empire. Theodosius I also decreed that those not believing in the Trinity were to be considered heretics. Five years later, this pronouncement resulted in the first case of

The Historical Perspective

capital punishment of a heretic. Priscillian, the Bishop of Avila in Spain, was executed. Unfortunately, Christianity had come full circle, and it was not until the Reformation that Christians began a steady but sure path of return to the basic teachings of Jesus.

Thus it was that Christianity, beginning with the missions of Paul, had spread from Jerusalem throughout the Near East, and finally to Rome. It was first adopted as the state religion by Armenia (north of Iran) in 301, by Ethiopia in 325, Georgia (later part of the Russian empire) in 325, and then the Roman Empire in 380. During the Middle Ages, Christianity expanded throughout the world. It survived persecutions, schisms and theological disputes, to become the world's largest religion.

Although Christians universally feel they have the answer, there is no general agreement as to how the new faith managed to spread so rapidly and successfully prior to Emperor Constantine. Rodney Stark, in his *The Rise of Christianity,* gives an in-depth review of the probable causes. Possibly, the social organization of its adherents, which undoubtedly improved the quality of their life, was a major factor. Stark's viewpoint is interesting in that, contrary to popular belief, he believes Christianity was a movement of the upper and middle classes, and not the lower, oppressed classes. And it took place in the cities. One additional point, the significance of which may have been overlooked even by Stark, is that pagan religions were primarily religions of men, while women were valued and allowed to participate in Christian worship. The men stayed home. The women regularly attended Christian services, and the women exercised a great deal of influence over their children, who undoubtedly became Christians as well. The best example of this theory may well be the Roman Emperor Constantine—his mother was a devout Christian.

The Emperor Constantine was neither Roman nor Italian. He was a Serbian, as was his father, a high-ranking Roman military commander and later, emperor. Serbia had been long under Roman rule, and as was the custom, which led to the success of the Roman Empire, citizens of conquered territories were immediately given a choice to cooperate. If they did so, they became Roman citizens, with rights equal to those in Rome, and many rose to become emperor, as did Constantine and his father.

Constantine, whose full name was Flavius Valerius Constantinus, was born in the city of Naissus (now Nis) in what is now known as Serbia, in the year 272. It is one of the oldest cities in Europe, and has from ancient times been a gateway between the East and the West. Five roads met at Naissus. They came from Lissus (in Albania), Serdica (Sophia, Bulgaria), Singidunum (Belgrade, now the capital of Serbia), Ratiaria (in northwestern Bulgaria) and Thessalonica (the second largest city in Greece). The city developed into an important Roman garrison town because of its strategic location.

In the year 268 AD, the Roman Empire came under severe attack from the Goths who crossed the Danube and ravaged the countryside. Claudius II finally defeated the Goths at Naissus in one of the bloodiest battles of that century, leaving 50,000 dead Goths strewn about the fields around the city. Four years later, the Roman military commander Constantius Chlorus, 23 years of age, came through Naissus on one of the many campaigns against remaining marauding Goths. He ordered his army to pitch tents in the surrounding fields, then went to the town inn, which he probably knew well. He had been born into a peasant family in a small village just a few miles north. Until age seventeen, the simple farming life was all that he knew. Then he joined the Roman army, learned Latin and Greek, and six years later returned as commander of the local Roman forces. He was tall, slender, of fair complexion with grey-blue eyes, and made an impressive figure in his uniform with its plumed helmet and flowing red cape (Kousoulas, D. G., *The Life and Times of Constantine the Great*). He did not return to his tent that night, but slept with the innkeeper's daughter, Helena, a slender, beautiful blond girl barely 16 years old.

There must have been more than a passing attachment to the young maiden, as Constantius left with her father a pouch of coins and his own tribunal cape, with its silver buckle engraved with his initials and rank. Nine months later, Helena gave birth to a boy she named Constantine.

It was almost ten years later that Constantius

came through Naissus again, this time as governor of Dalmatia, a Roman province on the Adriatic significantly larger than present day Dalmatia. This time when he left, his son Constantine went with him, as did Constantine's mother, Helena, to live in the governor's mansion in Dalmatia. Both Helena and Constantine were illiterate, speaking only the native language of Dardanian, which was also the native language of Constantius. They were both given tutors, and entered into a rigorous education. Constantius eventually married Helena, and Constantine accompanied his father throughout many campaigns, including travels to the northern borders of the Empire in Britain and as far south as Alexandria in Egypt.

Constantine followed in the footsteps of his father, and became a power-sharing Roman Emperor, a member of a tetrarchy. In February 313, Constantine met with Licinius, also a member of the tetrarchy, in Milan where they developed the Edict of Milan. The edict provided that Christians would be allowed to follow the faith of their choosing (Bowder, Diana. *The Age of Constantine and Julian.* New York: Barnes & Noble, 1978). The Edict of Milan also provided that all confiscated churches would be returned as well as other provisions for previously persecuted Christians.

The debate whether Constantine adopted his mother's Christianity in his youth, or whether he adopted it gradually over the course of his life continues. But one thing is certain, Christians were now secure in their religion.

CHAPTER 14

The Quest for the Historical Jesus

The term "quest for the historical Jesus" describes scholarly movements operating under the premise that the New Testament does not give an accurate historical account of the life of Jesus. The biblical description of Jesus is then referred to as the Christ of Faith. The *Historical Jesus*, whom those scholars seek to describe, is presented as a figure substantially different from that presented in the gospels. Such scholars purport to examine evidence from diverse sources, including, and with great reliance upon apocryphal (non-canonical) sources, which are subjected to critical examination according to their quasi-scientific rules, to create their version of a true composite picture of Jesus.

Prior to the Reformation, and for some time thereafter, there could be no such thing as the Quest for the Historical Jesus. Any such attempts usually led directly to burning at the stake. The earliest attempts to define Jesus in strictly historical terms are best summarized by Albert Schweitzer (1875-1965), an Alsatian theologian, philosopher, physician, medical missionary and musician. This remarkable man held the degrees of Doctor of Philosophy, Doctor of Theology, and Doctor of Medicine, and was also an accomplished organist. He is best known as the founder of the Albert Schweitzer Hospital in French

JESUS OF NAZARETH

Equatorial Africa (now Gabon, in west central Africa). Schweitzer was a German-speaking Lutheran who was born at a time when Alsace was under control of Germany. He challenged the Quest for the Historical Jesus scholars who had appeared primarily in Germany during the 19th Century. His monumental work, *The Quest of the Historical Jesus*, first published in German in 1906, was translated into English in 1910. As set forth in the Preface by the translator, the "book here translated is offered to the English-speaking public in the belief that it sets before them, as no other book has ever done, the history of the struggle which the best-equipped intellects of the modern world have gone through in endeavoring to realize for themselves the historical personality of our Lord."

Schweitzer reviewed all the former works on the "historical Jesus" back to the late 18th century. It is an interesting book to read, as Schweitzer shows us that the attempts to portray the historical Jesus were primarily attempts to discount the biblical narratives through explanations for the miracles and Divine Nature of Jesus as nothing more than the practice of a magician, or the result of other natural laws. Schweitzer does give a good historical account of the Quest movement, however, and he shows that the image of Jesus had changed with the times and outlooks of the various authors. In the final analysis, Schweitzer maintained that the life of Jesus must be interpreted in the light of Jesus' own convictions. In the following edited quotation from his book,

The Historical Perspective

Schweitzer concludes that:

"There is nothing more negative than the result of the critical study of the Life of Jesus. The Jesus of Nazareth who came forward publicly as the Messiah, who preached the ethic of the Kingdom of God, who founded the Kingdom of Heaven upon earth, and died to give His work its final consecration, never had any existence. He is a figure designed by rationalism, endowed with life by liberalism, and clothed by modern theology in an historical garb. This image has not been destroyed from without, it has fallen to pieces, cleft and disintegrated by the concrete historical problems which came to the surface one after another, and in spite of all the artifice, art, artificiality, and violence which was applied to them, refused to be planed down to fit the design on which the Jesus of the theology of the last hundred and thirty years had been constructed. Whatever the ultimate solution may be, the historical Jesus of the future can never render modern theology the services which it claimed from its own half-historical, half-modern, Jesus. He will be a Jesus, who was Messiah, and lived as such, either on the ground of a literary fiction of the earliest Evangelist, or on the ground of a purely eschatological [here, Divine] Messianic conception. In either case, He will not be a Jesus Christ to whom the religion of the present can ascribe, according to its long-cherished custom, its own thoughts and ideas, as it did with the Jesus of its own making. Nor will He be a figure which can be made, by a popular historical treatment, sympathetic and universally intelligible to the multitude. The historical Jesus will be to our time a stranger and an enigma. The study of the Life of Jesus has had a curious history. It set out in quest of the historical Jesus, believing that when it had found Him it could bring Him straight into our time as a Teacher and Saviour. It loosed the bands by which He had been riveted for centuries to the stony rocks of ecclesiastical doctrine, and rejoiced to see life and movement coming into the figure once more, and the historical Jesus advancing, as it seemed, to meet it. But He does not stay; He passes by our time and returns to His own. What surprised and dismayed the theology of the last forty years was that, despite all forced and arbitrary interpretations, it could not keep Him in our time, but had to let Him go. He returned to His own time, not owing to the application of any historical ingenuity, but by the same inevitable necessity by which the liberated pendulum returns to its original position. The historical foundation of Christianity as built up by rationalistic, by liberal, and by modern theology no longer exists; but that does not mean that Christianity has lost its historical foundation. The work which historical theology thought itself bound to carry out, and which fell to pieces just as it was nearing completion, was only the brick facing of the real immovable historical foundation which is independent of any historical confirmation or justification. Jesus means something to our world because a mighty spiritual force streams forth from Him and flows through our time also. This fact can

The Historical Perspective

neither be shaken nor confirmed by any historical discovery. It is the solid foundation of Christianity. The mistake was to suppose that Jesus could come to mean more to our time by entering into it as a man like ourselves. That is not possible. First because such a Jesus never existed. Secondly because, although historical knowledge can no doubt introduce greater clearness into an existing spiritual life, it cannot call spiritual life into existence.

"But the truth is, it is not Jesus as historically known, but Jesus as spiritually arisen within men, who is significant for our time and can help it. Not the historical Jesus, but the spirit which goes forth from Him and in the spirits of men strives for new influence and rule, is that which overcomes the world. The abiding and eternal in Jesus is absolutely independent of historical knowledge and can only be understood by contact with His spirit which is still at work in the world. In proportion as we have the Spirit of Jesus we have the true knowledge of Jesus.

"Modern Lives of Jesus are too general in their scope. They aim at influencing, by giving a complete impression of the life of Jesus, a whole community. But the historical Jesus, as He is depicted in the Gospels, influenced individuals by the individual word. They understood Him so far as it was necessary for them to understand, without forming any of His life as a whole, since this in its ultimate aims remained a mystery even for the disciples.

"He comes to us as One unknown, without a name, as of old, by the lakeside, He came to those men who knew Him not. He speaks to us the same word: 'Follow thou me!' and sets us to the tasks which He has to fulfill for our time. He commands. And to those who obey Him, whether they be wise or simple, He will reveal Himself in the toils, the conflicts, the sufferings which they shall pass through in His fellowship, and, as an ineffable mystery, they shall learn in their own experience Who He is." (Albert Schweitzer, *The Quest of the Historical Jesus*: First Complete Edition, trans. W. Montgomery, et al., ed. John Bowden, Fortress Press, 2001).

For Schweitzer, the senseless, useless quest for a historical Jesus beyond what is written in Scripture deserved the reproach: "he who putteth his hand to the plough, and looketh back, is not fit for the Kingdom of God" [Luke 9:62, King James Version].

CHAPTER 15

The Current Quest for the Historical Jesus

Notwithstanding the conclusion of Albert Schweitzer, the search goes on with renewed interest. The popular Jesus Seminar, a group of about 150 scholars and laymen founded in 1985, conducts an in-depth review of sources regarding the life of Jesus and his times, and decides upon a collective view of the "historicity" of the accounts by voting beads. The color of the bead represents how sure the person is that a saying or act was authentic. Here is how it works:

> Red beads – indicate that the voter believes Jesus did say what the passage claimed, or something very much like it. (3 Points)

> Pink beads – indicates Jesus probably said something like the passage. (2 Points)

> Grey beads – indicates that Jesus did not say the passage, but it contains Jesus' ideas. (1 Point)

> Black beads – mean that Jesus did not say the passage—it comes from later admirers or a different tradition. (0 Points)

JESUS OF NAZARETH

The group produced a new translation of its own version of the New Testament and apocrypha for use as textual sources. Members of the Jesus Seminar also run a series of workshops and give lectures in various American towns and cities, and they have published their major conclusions in three books: *The Five Gospels* (1993), *The Acts of Jesus* (1998) and *The Gospel of Jesus* (1999).

According to the Jesus Seminar, Jesus was simply a mortal man born of two human parents. He did not perform miracles or die as a substitute for sinners, nor rise bodily from the dead. As was proposed by those earlier quest scholars reviewed by Albert Schweitzer, the sightings of a risen Jesus after his crucifixion were nothing more than the visionary experiences of some of his disciples rather than actual physical encounters. The Seminar quite simply portrays Jesus as an itinerant Jewish sage and faith healer of peasant stock who preached a gospel of liberation from injustice.

The most prominent member of the Jesus Seminar is its co-founder, John Dominic Crossen, born in Ireland in 1934. He is an Irish-American religious scholar, former Catholic priest, and a best-selling author. The first book to bring him major recognition was *The Historical Jesus: The Life of a Mediterranean Jewish Peasant* (1991), eventually followed by *The Birth of Christianity: Discovering What Happened Immediately after the Execution of Jesus* (1998). He has written other books and essays, and lectured widely.

The Historical Perspective

Crossen's primary theme is that Jesus was an illiterate Jewish Cynic and that his ancestors and parents were landless peasants. The Cynic philosophy was that the purpose of life was to live a life of virtue in agreement with nature. This meant rejecting all conventional desires for wealth, power, health, and fame, and by living a simple life free from all possessions. Crossen believes that Jesus was a follower of John the Baptist, that Jesus was a healer of psychosomatic symptoms, and a man of great wisdom and courage who taught a message of tolerance and liberation. Crossen takes the position that many of the gospel stories of Jesus are not factual, including the raising of Lazarus, and that his virgin birth is fiction. But he does believe that Jesus was known during the earliest times as a powerful magician.

The gospels were never intended by their authors to be taken literally, according to Crossan, and he maintains that the meanings of the stories are what is important, not whether any particular narrative about Jesus is history or merely parable. Crossan states that the historical probability is that Jesus' body was scavenged by birds and animals, rather than being placed in a tomb at all. What he believes is difficult to fathom, but he apparently believes in some abstract concept of resurrection or affirmation by faith, and that resurrection of the body intact was never contemplated by the early Christians.

Crossan presents arguments based upon his concept of authentication to support his theology, if one can call it a theology. His books are complicated and difficult to follow, and he spends a great deal of time in evaluating the materials presented under his complicated scheme of cross-attestation.

Not only is the resurrection a piece of fiction, it is immaterial. Instead, Crossan maintains, what is important is that the "divine meaning of life is incarnated in a certain way of living." It is the continuing incarnation of divine justice in other human beings.

CHAPTER 16

The Secret Gospel of Mark

The Gospel of Mark in the New Testament may well not be complete, either because it was not finished, or because parts of it were lost, as claimed by Crossan and members of the Jesus Seminar. The Secret Gospel of Mark is believed by Crossan to be those parts of Mark which were intentionally suppressed or accidently lost to the world. Now that it has been "discovered" it is accepted by Crossan and given more weight than the canonical version of the Gospel of Mark.

The "Secret Gospel of Mark" was found in the library of a remote monastery near Jerusalem in 1958, according to Morton Smith, the person who "discovered" it (Morton Smith, *Clement of Alexandria and a Secret Gospel of Mark,* Harvard University Press. 1973). The missing parts of Mark were copied, supposedly, into the body of a letter from Clement of Alexandria found in the monastery of Mar Saba, on the West Bank. The letter is written to one Theodore, and in it Clement states that "Secret Mark" gives a more spiritual version of Mark. Clement sets out, in full, two passages from Secret Mark in his letter to Theodore, while warning him that other passages are false. Clement then endorses these two passages as complete and authentic verses missing from the Gospel of Mark.

To complicate the problem of authentication of the Clement letter, it is not the letter itself which was found, but a copy of the letter, which was transcribed into the back pages of another manuscript in the library. Thus, we have purportedly missing verses from Mark copied into a letter, which itself was copied into the back of another manuscript

The first verse of this previously unknown version of Mark is a highly suspect narrative of the raising of a boy from the dead by Jesus, somewhat analogous to the resurrection of Lazarus. According to the Clement letter, it is to be inserted between Mark 10:34 and 10:35. As translated by Morton Smith, that verse of Secret Mark reads as follows:

"And they come into Bethany. And a certain woman whose brother had died was there. And, coming, she prostrated herself before Jesus and says to him, 'Son of David, have mercy on me.' But the disciples rebuked her. And Jesus, being angered, went off with her into the garden where the tomb was, and straightway a great cry was heard from the tomb. And going near Jesus rolled away the stone from the door of the tomb. And straightway, going in where the youth was, he stretched forth his hand and raised him, seizing his hand. But the youth, looking upon him, loved him and began to beseech him that he might be with him. And going out of the tomb they came into the house of the youth, for he was rich. And after six days Jesus told him what to do and in the evening the youth comes to him, wearing a linen cloth over his naked body. And he remained with him that night, for Jesus taught him the mystery of the kingdom of God. And thence, arising, he returned to the other side of the Jordan."

In his letter, Clement then cautions Theodore that: "After these follows the text, 'And James and John come to him (Mark 10:35),' and all that section. But naked with naked, and the other things about which you wrote are not found."

The second excerpt from Secret Mark is very brief. According to the Clement letter, "And after the [words] 'And he comes into Jericho' (Mark 10:46) [the Secret Gospel] adds only, 'And the sister of the youth whom Jesus loved and his mother and Salome were there, and Jesus did not receive them.' But the many other [things about] which you wrote both seem to be and are falsifications."

After Smith's belated announcement in 1973 of his earlier finding in 1958, the manuscript containing the Clement letter was located at Mar Saba, and then transferred to the Greek Orthodox Patriarchate library in Jerusalem for further study. While there, the copy of the letter containing Secret Mark was cut out of the back of the old manuscript in which it was copied, and photographed by the librarian. After that, it mysteriously disappeared. No one has been able to locate the letter since. All that we now have are black and white photographs made by Morton Smith in 1958, and color photographs made by the librarian in Jerusalem in 1976.

As might be expected, the revelation of this otherwise unknown letter created a sensation at the time of its "discovery," because "Secret Mark" suggests in very explicit language that Jesus had a homosexual relationship with a boy he raised from the dead. But in 2001 it became apparent that Morton Smith's discovery was remarkably similar to the plot in a novel by Canadian writer James H. Hunter, the title of which was *The Mystery of Mar Saba*, published in 1940, just two years before Smith's visit to that monastery, when he was trapped at the library during World War II while doing an inventory of the manuscripts. In that mystery novel, a German archeologist attempted to plant a hoax manuscript embarrassing to Christianity in the Mar Saba library, but was unmasked by an American.

The similarities between the novel and the claims by Morton Smith, who was stranded at the Mar Saba library shortly after Hunter's fictional account was published, led most scholars to regard the discovery as a hoax and to dismiss it outright.

After Morton Smith's death, Jacob Neusner, a professor and specialist in ancient Judaism, and a former student of Morton Smith, denounced the alleged Secret Gospel of Mark as the "forgery of the century." Neusner never offered any further explanation for his statement, and that is probably because no further comment was warranted. Neusner is well

The Historical Perspective

respected in academic circles, and has been quoted favorably by the current Pope in regard to other matters such as "Rabbi Neusner's conversation with the Jesus of the Sermon on the Mount" (Ratzinger, Joseph. *Jesus of Nazareth,* pp. 303-304).

However, Crossan accepts Secret Mark as authentic based upon his research. In discussing his method of research into the historical Jesus, Crossan, states that:

"My methodology for Jesus research has a triple triadic process: the campaign, the strategy, and the tactics, as it were. The first triad involves the reciprocal interplay of a macrocosmic level using cross-cultural and cross-temporal social anthropology, a mesocosmic level using Hellenistic or Greco-Roman history, and a microcosmic level using the literature of specific sayings and doings, stories and anecdotes, confessions and interpretations concerning Jesus. All three levels, anthropological, historical, and literary, must cooperate fully and equally for an effective synthesis. Let me insist on and underline that point. I presume an equal and interactive cooperation in which weakness in any element imperils the integrity and validity of the others. (Crossan, John Dominic, *The Historical Jesus: The Life of a Mediterranean Jewish Peasant*, Harper Collins, 1991)."

Finally, Crossan gives Secret Mark his stamp of approval and says: "First, canonical Mark is a censored version of Secret Mark...." How he arrived at that conclusion, or how his method of research validates Secret Mark remains a mystery. Nevertheless, Crossan then cites Secret Mark as authority that Mark also contains a parallel miracle of raising a man from the dead, as is reported in John with the resurrection of Lazarus. Thus, it appears that Crossan believes Secret Mark to be part of the original Mark, that it was removed because of censorship, and that it speaks with more authority than the canonical Mark of the New Testament.

It is unfortunate that such an important document can not be found so that it can be subjected to scientific ink analysis to establish whether or not the Clement letter is a forgery, made either by Morton Smith himself or some other person.

In conclusion, regarding the Quest for the Historical Jesus, if one thinks such a trip is really necessary, it is possible to spend several hours, if not days and months, pursuing books on the subject and articles in the Journal for the Study of the Historical Jesus, and arrive absolutely nowhere. Eventually one comes full circle and finally finds himself comfortable with the conclusion reached by Albert Schweitzer more than a hundred years ago: "The mistake was to suppose that Jesus could come to mean more to our time by entering into it as a man like ourselves."

CHAPTER 17

The Divine Jesus
by
Benjamin Rush Rhees (edited)

Jesus stands before us as a man, conscious of his close kinship with his fellows. Like them he hungered and thirsted and grew weary. Like them he longed for friendship and for sympathy. Like them he trusted God and prayed to God and learned still to trust when his request was denied. He stands before us also as a man conscious of being anointed by God for the great work which all the prophets had foretold, and of being fully equipped with authority and power and the promise of unapproachable dignity. Of deep religious spirit and great reverence for the scriptures of his people, he yet used these scriptures as a master does his tools, to serve his work rather than for self instruction. He drew his knowledge from within and from above, and proclaimed his own fulfillment of the scriptures when he filled them with new meaning. A man always devout, always at prayer, he is never seen, like Isaiah, prostrate before the Most High, crying, "I am undone" (Isaiah 6:5). In his moments of greatest seriousness and most manifest communion with heaven he looked to God as his nearest of kin, and felt himself a stranger on the earth fulfilling his Father's will. He felt heaven to be his home not simply by God's gracious promise, but by the right of previous possession.

The miracles with which the gospels have filled the record of Jesus' life have caused perplexity to many. They belong with those other mysterious things recorded for us in the story of the past. And they all pale before the unaccountable exception to universal human experience presented by this Man of Nazareth. It confronts us when we think of the un-schooled Jew who, in his thought of God, rose not only above all of his generation, but higher than all who had gone before or come after him, one who built on the foundation of the past a superstructure of religion new, and simple, and clearly heavenly. It confronts us when we think of this Man who believed that it was given to him to establish the kingdom that should fill the whole earth, and who had the boldness and the faith to ignore the opposition of all the world's wisdom and of all its enthroned power, and to fulfill his task as the woman does who hides her leaven in the meal, content to wait for years, or millenniums, until his truth shall conquer in the re-alization of God's will on earth even as it is done in heaven. It confronts us when we consider that the Man who has shown his brethren what obedience means, who has taught them to pray, who has been for all these centuries the Way, the Truth, the Life, by whom they come to God, habitually claimed with-out shadow of abashment or slightest hint of con-scious presumption, a nature, a relation to God, a freedom from sin, that other men according to the measure of their godliness would shun as blasphemy. Jesus of the gospels is the exception to the uniform fact of human nature. Paul, whose life was transformed and his thinking revolutionized by his meeting with the risen Jesus, thought on these things and believed that "the name which, is above every name" was his by right of nature as well as by the reward of obedience (Phil. 2:5-11). John came to believe that he whom he had seen with his eyes, heard with his ears, handled with his hands, was, indeed, "the Word made flesh" (John 1:14), through whom God revealed his love to men.

Through all the perplexities of doubt, amidst all the irrelevant speculations, the hearts of men today turn to this Jesus of Nazareth as their supreme revelation of God, and find in him "the Master of their thinking and the Lord of their lives." "Lord, to whom shall we go? You have the words of eternal life. And we have believed and know that you are the Holy One of God."

AFTERWORD

By the 1950's the portrayal of the "Historical Jesus" and the "Christ of Faith" had developed such divergent views that the man Jesus could no longer fit into the concept of Jesus as the Son of the living God. The two views of Jesus were incompatible. The authors of the various modern works on the Historical Jesus developed a man more like a man of our times than antiquity, and often resembling more the self image of the author than a holy man of the Bible.

Many Christians, feeling their faith under attack, retreated further and further into the traditional concepts of Jesus Christ as developed through the centuries. A further group of dispirited Christians felt themselves "in danger of clutching at thin air" as the Christ of their faith retreated before the onslaught of so-called experts and "scholars." Many steadfast Christians buried their heads in the sand and ignored the turmoil around them, while others simply left the Church and never looked back.

The historical setting, the historical perspective, as is the sub-title of this book, is indispensible to a true understanding of the Christ of Faith and the accounts of the gospels. Jesus of Nazareth existed as a real man in a historical setting—the gospels are intertwined with real historical events. None of the historical facts illuminated in this book should oper-

The Historical Perspective

ate to diminish one's faith, but only to increase faith
through a truer understanding of the world as it existed at the time Jesus walked upon the earth.

Through the years, clerics and others have taken
the liberty to expound upon scripture, interpret
scripture, or simply selectively redact scripture, to
achieve the purpose of the scribe, who doubtless
meant well. We have no original manuscripts of the
gospels or other scripture. It is simply not possible
for parchment or papyrus to survive for that length
of time without environmental controls. What we
have are copies of copies of copies of copies, etc., all
meticulously made by hand under the light of oil
lamps in damp monastic libraries, with the oldest
manuscripts dating back to the Fourth Century.
From time to time, older version of one or another
passages from the Bible were found, carefully scruti-
nized by experts, and either accepted, leading to a re-
vised version of the Bible, or rejected as not authentic or outright frauds. It is not a field for amateurs.

Some innocent Christian redactions may have
done more harm than good. An example is that of
Barabbas. At one point, the oral and written traditions upon which the gospels are based referred to
this insurrectionist by his full name, Jesus bar-
Abbas, Jesus the Son of the Father. When referring
to God, his father, Jesus of Nazareth used the Aramaic word "Abba." Apparently, "abba" could also
mean father in the common sense, as well as Rabbi.
Later scribes omitted the name Jesus from the name
of Barabbas so as not to diminish the status of Jesus

of Nazareth. As a result, the scene before Pilate is portrayed as the Jewish masses electing to free some common criminal named Barabbas in lieu of our Lord, for no logical or understandable reason other than that the Jews wanted to do Christ harm and that they wanted the world to remember that Christ's "blood was upon their hands."

How much more comforting it is to learn from earlier copies of Scripture that the full name of the man Pilate pardoned was Jesus bar Abbas. The followers of Jesus of Nazareth had fled into hiding, and the remaining Jewish masses could have been mislead by the chief priests, those Sadducees, hand picked by Rome, who had little use for religion in any form, and who recognized Jesus of Nazareth as the real threat to their power. As for God's plan, should one need to search for such, what better measure to ensure that Scripture is fulfilled than to bring before the public a fraud for the priests to point out as the one to be saved from crucifixion.

Therefore, if we want to understand Scripture in the spirit in which it was written, we must return to the times and events during which it was written, using the earliest and most reliable manuscripts available. If one does so, perhaps one will discover Jesus in a new light, the vision he had of himself.

A great many people of the current generation do not believe Jesus actually existed. But there is abundant, irrefutable non-Biblical evidence that he did, and that he was executed by the Romans through or-

The Historical Perspective

der of Pontius Pilate, acting according to the wishes of those members of the Jewish elite anxious to remain in power as puppets of Rome.

After his crucifixion something happened that shook the foundation of the world. Although the various accounts are confusing as to who first saw the risen Christ and where, something undoubtedly happened. Peter, who was in hiding along with other Apostles, suddenly becomes solid as a "rock." No longer cringing in the dark, he stands up for Jesus, enters upon a mission, and eventually submits to the same fate as Christ, crucifixion at Rome. James, the brother of Jesus, no longer doubts, but becomes the leader of the Church at Jerusalem.

If this were a fraudulent scheme cooked up by the Apostles, one would expect that at the least they would get their stories straight. But the discrepancies in the accounts speak more for the credibility of the empty tomb than had each account been precisely the same in every detail, as is well known to students of trials in the courts.

Again in Acts, Luke tells us that Jesus had shown himself alive to the Apostles many times over a period of forty days, and he tells of Paul's conversion on the road to Damascus. In 1 Corinthians 15, Paul states that Jesus first appeared to Peter and secondly to the Twelve, then to more than five hundred brothers, most of whom were still alive at the time; then he appeared to James (the brother of the Lord). Paul concludes his recounting of the resurrection by saying: "If there is no resurrection of the dead, Christ himself cannot have been raised, and if Christ has not been raised then our preaching is useless and your believing it is useless; indeed, we are shown up as witnesses who have committed perjury before God.... If our hope in Christ has been for this life only, we are the most unfortunate people. But Christ has in fact been raised from the dead...." This is what it is all about. Not the weight of Church tradition and mysticism gathered up through the centuries, but the simple fact that Christ is risen.

And his message was so compelling that Christianity spread like wildfire notwithstanding the difficulties of travel and the many months it took to communicate from city to city. In just 30 years after the crucifixion, there were so many Christians in Rome that Nero could blame them for the fire which destroyed the city.

Pax Domini

[Note: The term disciple is derived from the Greek word which means student. The disciples were the students of Jesus, and they consisted of a large number ranging from 70 to 120 and an even greater multitude according to the gospels and Acts. The word Apostle can best be translated as messenger, (Greek, *apostolos*, literally one sent forth—Vine Expository Dictionary of NT Words), and these were the disciples Jesus selected to be his inner circle who were given more specific instruction and sent out to convey the message of the "good news of the gospel of Jesus Christ," as is related in Matthew 10:5. The Book of Acts states that the Apostles themselves had disciples (students). According to Luke 10, Jesus appointed an additional 72 disciples as apostles and sent them out to all the towns and places he was to visit. Paul used the term apostle to refer to others than the original twelve, including his mentor, Barnabas (Acts 14:14).]

CPSIA information can be obtained at www.ICGtesting.com
Printed in the USA
BVOW070400170812

298030BV00001B/73/P